Heart Foundation

Deliciously Healthy

COOKBOOK

Heart Foundation

Deliciously Healthy

COOKBOOK

Food by Jody Vassallo   Photography by Louise Lister

ACKNOWLEDGMENTS

Food Writer   Jody Vassallo
Photographer   Louise Lister
Stylist   Janelle Bloom
Home Economist   Jody Vassallo
Designer   Annette Fitzgerald
Editor   Lynelle Scott-Aitken
Nutrition Copy Editor   Veronique Droulez
Styling Credit   Thanks to Breville Holdings Pty Ltd

HEART FOUNDATION TEAM

Project and Marketing Manager   Nicola Stewart
Nutrition Writer and Consultant   Vanessa Jones
Nutrition Consultant   Therese Abbey
Nutrition Editor   Susan Anderson
Nutrition Copy Contributors   Cathy Cooper,
Barbara Eden, Ernestine van Herwerden and
Jane Welsh

National Heart Foundation of Australia
ABN 98 008 419 761
PO Box 9966 in your capital city
Phone: 1300 55 02 82
Web: www.heartfoundation.com.au

Printed by R&R Publications Marketing Pty Ltd
(ACN 083 612 579) PO Box 254, Carlton North,
Victoria 3054 Australia Toll Free: 1800 063 296

Colour Separations by Color Gallery, Malaysia

**Heart
Foundation**

Enquiries should be made in writing to the
Heart Foundation, PO Box 2222, Strawberry Hills BC
NSW 2012. Phone: (02) 9219 2444
Email: NSW@heartfoundation.com.au

Heart Foundation Cookbook, Deliciously Healthy
ISBN 1740221435

Cover: Smoked Salmon, Asparagus and Lemon Fettuccine
(p96) Back cover: Chocolate Raspberry Brownies (p134)

Contents

We are delighted to present the new Heart Foundation Deliciously Healthy Cookbook, which is our response to the enthusiastic demand from our many supporters and the general public who have two goals: to enjoy eating well and to maintain a healthy heart. Our cookbook is bursting with delicious, healthy and easy-to-prepare recipes tailored to time-conscious individuals and families.

Every recipe is:

Nutritious - our recipes meet specific nutritional criteria set by the Heart Foundation including total fat, saturated fat, sodium (salt) and fibre. Every recipe has an analysis of nutrients per serve. (See page 154 for an explanation)

Tasty - eating should be a pleasurable experience so our recipes are extensively tested and sampled to ensure they are delicious as well as healthy. Our recipes are inspired by multicultural influences and traditional favourites.

Quick and easy - we all appreciate great food that is fast to prepare. Our recipes are quick and simple to make, and the ingredients are readily available.

HEALTHY EATING - Helping your heart

There are four key principles in heart disease prevention:

1 Healthy Fats - achieving a healthy balance between unsaturated fats (which reduce the risk of heart disease) and saturated fats (which increase the risk of heart disease).
2 Fish - studies have shown that people who eat fish at least twice a week are less likely to die from heart disease.
3 Wholegrain cereals, nuts, seeds, legumes, fruit and vegetables - plant-based foods are low in saturated fat and the following components found in them may also contribute to heart health:
◆ Dietary fibre in oats, barley, psyllium and legumes have been shown to reduce

cholesterol levels in the blood. High blood cholesterol increases the risk of developing heart disease.
◆ Folate in legumes, vegetables, wholegrain foods, fruit and nuts may reduce the level of an amino acid in the blood known as homocysteine. This may be beneficial since high levels of homocysteine in the blood is associated with an increased risk of cardiovascular disease.
◆ Antioxidants in fruit, vegetables and wholegrain foods may play a role in preventing the development of heart disease.
◆ Plant sterols (from 2g/day), found in all plant foods, have been shown to lower cholesterol levels in the blood.
4 Sodium - restricting sodium intake can help lower high blood pressure.

FATS - What's the difference?

Fats in food are a mixture of four types of fats: saturated fats, polyunsaturated fats, monounsaturated fats and trans fats. The risk of heart disease differs according to the type of fat:

1 Saturated fats increase the risk of heart disease. Diets high in saturated fat have been shown to raise undesirable total and LDL cholesterol in the blood.
2 Polyunsaturated fats reduce the risk of heart disease. They have been shown to lower undesirable total and LDL cholesterol in the blood.
a) Omega-3 polyunsaturated fats (DHA and EPA) are found predominantly in fish. They appear to prevent arrhythmia (a condition of irregular heart beats) which

can lead to sudden death or cardiac events.

b) Alpha-linolenic acid is a different type of omega-3 polyunsaturated fat, found in canola and soybean oils, which has been shown to lower blood cholesterol levels. Alpha-linolenic acid may play an important role in preventing heart disease.

3 Monounsaturated fats have been shown to lower undesirable total and LDL cholesterol, but not to the same extent as polyunsaturated fats.

4 Trans fats are mainly produced when vegetable oils are hydrogenated to produce margarine, deep-frying oils, biscuits and pastries. They have been shown to raise undesirable total and LDL cholesterol and lower healthy HDL cholesterol in the blood. Today, most margarine spreads in Australia are produced without trans fats.

ENJOY HEALTHY EATING
A guide to keeping your blood cholesterol in check

◆ Use margarine spreads instead of butter or dairy blends.

◆ Use a variety of oils for cooking - some suitable choices include canola, sunflower, soybean, olive and peanut oils.

◆ Use salad dressings and mayonnaise made from oils such as canola, sunflower, soybean and olive oils.

◆ Choose low or reduced fat milk and yoghurt or 'added calcium' soy beverages. Try to limit cheese and ice-cream to twice a week.

◆ Have fish (any type of fresh or canned) at least twice a week.

◆ Select lean meat (meat trimmed of fat and chicken without skin). Try to limit fatty meats including sausages and delicatessen meats such as salami.

◆ Snack on plain, unsalted nuts and fresh fruit.

◆ Incorporate dried peas (eg split peas), dried beans (eg haricot beans, kidney beans), canned beans (eg baked beans, three bean mix) or lentils into two meals a week.

◆ Base your meals around vegetables and grain based foods such as breakfast cereals, bread, pasta, noodles and rice.

◆ Try to limit take-away foods to once a week. Take-away foods include pastries, pies, pizza, hamburgers and creamy pasta dishes.

◆ Try to limit snack foods such as potato crisps and corn crisps to once a week.

◆ Try to limit cakes, pastries and chocolate or creamy biscuits to once a week.

◆ Try to limit cholesterol-rich foods such as egg yolks and offal eg liver, kidney and brains.

Lowering your sodium intake
Healthy adults need less than 2300 mg of sodium a day to balance the amount of fluid in the body and maintain muscle and nerve function. Excess sodium in the diet is linked to high blood pressure.

Which oil is best?

Use a variety of different oils to prepare and cook quick, great tasting meals. Oils such as canola, sunflower, soybean, olive, peanut, macadamia, sesame seed and grapeseed are all suitable.

Isn't too much fat bad for the heart?

The type of fat, rather than the amount of fat has been shown to be a major factor determining the risk of heart disease. Saturated fat is the type of fat, which increases your blood cholesterol level and increases your risk of heart disease. Focus on reducing your intake of foods high in saturated fat such as fatty meats, full cream dairy products, butter, two vegetable oils - coconut and palm oil, most deep fried take-aways and commercially baked products such as biscuits and pastries.

Should I eat less meat and dairy foods?

Lean red meat, trimmed of visible fat, is low in saturated fat. It is an excellent source of iron, zinc and vitamin B12 and plays an important role in healthy eating. It is very important to limit the amount of full fat dairy products you eat. Full fat dairy products are a major source of saturated fat. Low or reduced fat dairy products are major sources of calcium in the Australian diet. Calcium plays an important role in preventing the development of osteoporosis.

Is wine good for the heart?

Alcohol doesn't raise blood cholesterol but it can raise blood triglycerides, blood pressure and body weight. One or two drinks a day may do you no harm, but excessive drinking increases your risk of high blood pressure, heart disease and stroke, as well as many other problems.

The main source of excess sodium is salt: both table salt and salt added to processed foods. One teaspoon of table salt alone provides 2000 mg of sodium! The simplest ways to reduce sodium in your diet are to:

◆ Choose low salt or reduced salt food products where available.
◆ Flavour your meals with herbs and spices rather than salt.
◆ Eat less highly salted food, such as packet chips and other snack food, salty commercial sauces, processed meats and fish paste, soup and stock powders, stock cubes, pickles, highly preserved food and most takeaway food.

What about foods high in cholesterol, like eggs?

Cholesterol in food can raise cholesterol in the blood, particularly in people who have a high risk of developing heart disease. Cholesterol in food does not raise cholesterol in the blood to the same extent as saturated and trans fats. The Heart Foundation recommends that people at high risk of heart disease should restrict their intake of cholesterol-rich foods. People at low risk of heart disease can eat reasonable amounts of cholesterol-rich foods such as egg yolks and offal.

Heart Foundation

Getting the Balance Right

Enjoying a variety of foods from the different food groups is the key to healthy eating. Use this checklist to assess your current food intake and guide you towards a healthy eating pattern.

Food Group Checklist	Serves	Size per serve
Vegetables and legumes (pulses)	5 or more serves a day	1/2 cup cooked vegetables OR 1 cup salad vegetables OR 1/2 cup cooked legumes (dried beans, lentils or chickpeas)
Fruit	2 or more serves a day	1 medium piece fruit (eg 1 apple) OR 2 small pieces fruit (eg 2 kiwifruit) OR 1 cup diced or canned fruit OR 1 1/2 tablespoons dried fruit OR 4 dried apricot halves OR 1/2 cup fruit juice
Bread, cereals, rice, pasta and noodles	4 or more serves a day	2 slices bread OR 1 medium bread roll OR 1 cup cooked porridge OR 1 1/3 cups ready to eat cereal OR 1/2 cup untoasted muesli OR 1 cup cooked rice, pasta, noodles OR 1/3 cup flour. Of the recommended 4 or more serves a day, aim to eat at least 1 serve of wholegrain breads and cereals (eg wholemeal bread, wholegrain breakfast cereals, brown rice, wholemeal pasta)
◆Low or reduced fat dairy products OR calcium enriched soy products	2-3 serves a day	1 cup low or reduced fat milk OR 1 cup calcium enriched soy drink OR 2 slices (40g) low or reduced fat cheese OR 1 small carton (200g) low or reduced fat yoghurt OR 1 cup low or reduced fat custard
◆Fish and shellfish	At least 2 fish meals a week.	100g to150g cooked fish OR 1 cup shellfish (shelled)
◆Lean red or white meat, poultry, eggs, nuts and legumes	Lean meat or poultry: 3-4 serves a week. Legumes: 1-2 serves a week (dried beans, lentils, chickpeas). Nuts: 2 serves a week. Eggs: up to one per day if your blood cholesterol is normal. Eat fewer egg yolks if your blood cholesterol level is high	80-120g cooked lean meat or poultry 1/2 cup cooked legumes 1/3 cup nuts 48-50g egg size
Margarine spreads, oils, mayonnaise and salad dressing	1-2 serves a day	1 tablespoon

◆ Vegetarians should substitute appropriate non-animal foods for animal foods as required.

Breakfast, Snacks and Lunch

Making healthy food choices can be a challenge if you're running late for work or only have a few minutes to spare for a snack. So stock up on some of our fast, fresh ideas and save yourself the worry.

NUTRIENTS per serve

Energy	1818kJ
Energy	434cal
Total fat	12.0g
Saturated fat	1.6g
Monounsaturated fat	6.5g
Polyunsaturated fat	3.0g
Protein	14.0g
Carbohydrate	68.0g
Fibre	10.0g
Sodium	62mg
Cholesterol	5.5mg

TIP

The Heart Foundation recommends eating a variety of breads and cereals. This food group is an important source of carbohydrate, dietary fibre and a wide variety of vitamins and minerals, including folate, thiamin, riboflavin, niacin and iron. The current guidelines in Australia recommend adults eat at least 4 serves of bread, cereals, rice, pasta or noodles each day.

NUTRIENTS per serve

Energy	963kJ
Energy	230cal
Total fat	4.8g
Saturated fat	0.7g
Monounsaturated fat	1.0g
Polyunsaturated fat	2.7g
Protein	6.2g
Carbohydrate	41.0g
Fibre	1.6g
Sodium	239mg
Cholesterol	31mg

Bircher Muesli

PREP TIME 10 minutes + 1 hour standing   COOKING TIME Nil

1 apple, peeled cored and grated
1 pear, peeled, cored and grated
2 cups rolled oats
1/2 teaspoon ground cinnamon
250ml pear juice
150g reduced fat vanilla yoghurt

50g toasted flaked almonds
250ml reduced fat milk
2 mangoes, peeled and chopped
1 banana, sliced
2 passionfruit

1 Put the apple, pear, rolled oats, cinnamon and pear juice in a bowl and mix to combine, allow to stand covered in the refrigerator for 1 hour.
2 Fold through the yoghurt and almonds. Spoon the muesli into individual bowls and serve topped with the milk, mango and banana then drizzle with passionfruit pulp.
Serves 4

Apple Cinnamon Muffins

PREP TIME 15 minutes   COOKING TIME 30 minutes

canola cooking spray
200g canned pie apple
1 teaspoon ground cinnamon
2 1/2 cups self-raising flour
1 cup rolled oats
2/3 cup brown sugar
375ml low or reduced fat milk

2 eggs, lightly beaten
1 teaspoon vanilla essence
2 tablespoons safflower oil
100g thick, reduced fat vanilla yoghurt
2 tablespoons brown sugar, extra
2 tablespoons rolled oats, extra

1 Preheat oven to 200°C. Spray 12 small (125 ml) muffin tins with canola spray.
2 Put the pie apple in a bowl, stir in half the cinnamon and set aside.
3 Sift the flour and remaining cinnamon into a large bowl, stir in the rolled oats and brown sugar. Make a well in the centre.
4 Put the milk, eggs, vanilla essence, oil and yoghurt in a jug and whisk to combine.
5 Pour the liquid ingredients into the well and mix until just combined - do not over mix - the mixture should still be lumpy. Over mixing will also make the muffins tough.
6 Half fill the muffin tins with the muffin mixture, place half a tablespoon of the apple mixture into each hole, then top with the remaining muffin mixture.
7 Sprinkle with the brown sugar and rolled oats. Bake for 25-30 minutes or until the muffins are risen and have started to come away from the side of the tin. Allow to cool for 5 minutes in their tins before turning out onto a wire rack to cool completely. Makes 12

Jumbo Pancakes with Blackberry and Honey

PREP TIME **25 minutes** COOKING TIME **20 minutes**

1¹/2 cups self-raising flour
¹/2 cup wholemeal self-raising flour
1 teaspoon baking powder
2 tablespoons caster sugar
1 egg, lightly beaten
2 egg whites
375ml buttermilk

200g blackberries
40g reduced fat polyunsaturated
    margarine
canola cooking spray
50g macadamia nuts, toasted
¹/4 cup honey

1 Sift the flours and baking powder into a large bowl, stir in the sugar. Make a well in the centre. Add the combined egg, egg whites and buttermilk and whisk until the mixture forms a smooth batter. Cover and allow to stand while preparing the butter.
2 To make the blackberry butter, put half the blackberries and the margarine in a bowl and mix gently to combine, taking care not to puree the blackberries.
3 Heat a non stick fry pan over medium heat and coat lightly with canola spray. Pour ¹/4 cup of the batter into the pan and swirl gently to distribute the pancake mixture. Cook until bubbles appear on the surface and the underside is golden. Turn and cook the other side until cooked through. Keep warm and cook the remaining batter.
4 Chop the nuts, put in a bowl and stir with honey to combine.
5 Serve pancake stacks topped with a generous dollop of blackberry butter and a spoonful of macadamia nut honey. Sprinkle with the remaining blackberries.
Serves 4

NUTRIENTS per serve

Energy	2336kJ
Energy	558cal
Total fat	18.0g
Saturated fat	3.9g
Monounsaturated fat	10.0g
Polyunsaturated fat	2.6g
Protein	16.0g
Carbohydrate	83.0g
Fibre	7.6g
Sodium	621mg
Cholesterol	54mg

TIP

Buttermilk is an excellent substitute for milk or cream because it has a reduced fat content. It is made from pasteurised skim milk, tastes mildly acidic and has a thick consistency similar to that of drinking yoghurt. Cakes made with buttermilk have a deliciously moist texture.

STAR INGREDIENT

BLACKBERRIES are not true berries but aggregates of several small fruit. They are a good source of dietary fibre, vitamins C and E, and contribute small quantities of many other vitamins and minerals. Eat them sweet and fresh as a snack or lightly stewed for dessert.

Berry Couscous with Maple Syrup

PREP TIME 5 minutes + 10 minutes standing COOKING TIME 5 minutes

1 cup couscous
1/2 cup dried cranberries
500ml raspberry cranberry juice
200g strawberries, halved
150g blueberries
150g raspberries

1 tablespoon chopped fresh mint
   (optional)
200g reduced fat vanilla yoghurt
2 tablespoons sunflower seeds
2 tablespoons pepitas
2 tablespoons maple syrup

1 Put the couscous and dried cranberries in a bowl. Heat the raspberry cranberry juice in a pot until it comes to the boil, pour over the couscous and allow to stand for 10 minutes or until all the liquid has been absorbed.
2 Fold through the strawberries, blueberries, raspberries and mint if using.
3 Spoon the couscous into individual bowls and top with a generous dollop of yoghurt, sprinkle with the combined seeds and drizzle with maple syrup. Serves 4

If raspberry cranberry juice is not available try apple or pear juice instead.

NUTRIENTS per serve

Energy	2528kJ
Energy	604cal
Total fat	7.0g
Saturated fat	1.1g
Monounsaturated fat	1.4g
Polyunsaturated fat	3.8g
Protein	9.6g
Carbohydrate	98.0g
Fibre	6.6g
Sodium	74mg
Cholesterol	5mg

TIP

Oats and oat bran are very rich in soluble fibre, which has been shown to bind with and remove dietary cholesterol from the intestinal tract. Therefore eating food high in soluble fibre may assist in reducing blood cholesterol levels over time. So eat plenty of foods rich in soluble fibre including oats, vegetables, legumes, cereals and fresh or dried fruit.

High Fibre Power Porridge

PREP TIME 10 minutes COOKING TIME 10 minutes

2 cups rolled oats
2 tablespoons wheatgerm
2 tablespoons ground soy linseed mix
3 tablespoons sunflower seeds
zest of 1 orange
1/2 teaspoon mixed spice

250ml reduced fat milk
2 tablespoons soft brown sugar
4 sugar bananas, sliced
1/4 cup shelled pistachio nuts, chopped

1 Put the oats, wheatgerm, soy linseed mix, sunflower seeds, orange zest, mixed spice and 4 cups of water in a saucepan. Bring porridge to the boil, stirring occasionally, then reduce heat and simmer for 5-10 minutes or until the oats are soft and creamy.
2 Spoon the porridge into individual bowls, pour over the milk and sprinkle with the brown sugar. Top with sliced banana and pistachio nuts. Serves 4

NUTRIENTS per serve

Energy	1699kJ
Energy	406cal
Total fat	13.0g
Saturated fat	1.7g
Monounsaturated fat	5.0g
Polyunsaturated fat	5.7g
Protein	13.0g
Carbohydrate	59.0g
Fibre	7.9g
Sodium	34mg
Cholesterol	2mg

Skinny Eggs and Ham on Bagels

PREP TIME **20 minutes** COOKING TIME **5 minutes**

100g cherry tomatoes
12 fresh flat parsley leaves
canola cooking spray
4 eggs
4 egg whites

125ml reduced fat evaporated milk
ground white pepper to taste
2 wholemeal bagels, halved
100g shaved reduced fat ham

1 Cut the cherry tomatoes in half and place on a non stick baking tray. Grill until soft and the skins begin to shrink. Remove and keep warm.

2 Put the parsley leaves on another baking tray, lightly spray with the oil and grill until crisp.

3 Put the egg, egg whites and evaporated milk in a bowl, whisk to combine and season with a little white pepper.

4 Pour the egg mixture into a non stick fry pan and cook over a low heat until the egg starts to set. Stir gently until just cooked. Do not overcook or the texture will not be smooth.

5 Toast the bagels and top the bases with a little of the shaved ham, scrambled eggs, cherry tomatoes and crisp parsley leaves. Serves 4

NUTRIENTS per serve

Energy	1586kJ
Energy	379cal
Total fat	8.6g
Saturated fat	2.6g
Monounsaturated fat	3.0g
Polyunsaturated fat	1.6g
Protein	26.0g
Carbohydrate	48.0g
Fibre	6.4g
Sodium	989mg
Cholesterol	194mg

TIP

Only people with high blood cholesterol levels need to limit their intake of foods rich in dietary cholesterol. If your blood cholesterol level is high, limit your intake of egg yolks, offal (brains, kidneys, liver) and shellfish. If your blood cholesterol is normal, it is acceptable to enjoy these foods a little more often.

STAR INGREDIENT

TOMATOES are wonderfully versatile. They can be eaten fresh, canned, concentrated as paste, sun dried or used to make tomato sauce. They belong to the fruit family and used to be known as 'love apples'. Tomatoes are rich in vitamin C and carotene (which is converted into vitamin A) and are a good source of dietary fibre.

Fruit Bread Toast with Ricotta and Strawberries

PREP TIME 10 minutes COOKING TIME 5 minutes

1 loaf or 8 thick slices fruit bread
250g reduced fat ricotta cheese
1-2 tablespoons icing sugar
1/2 teaspoon vanilla essence

500g strawberries, halved
3 passionfruit, halved
2 tablespoons maple syrup

1 Toast the fruit bread slices until crisp and golden. Keep warm.
2 Put the ricotta, icing sugar and vanilla essence in a bowl and mix gently to combine.
3 Put the strawberries, passionfruit and maple syrup in a bowl and stir gently to coat the berries with syrup.
4 Put two slices of the toast on a plate, top with a generous dollop of the ricotta mixture and finish off with a couple of generous spoonfuls of the berry mix. Serves 4

This recipe is also delicious with a mix of either banana and passionfruit, or mango and passionfruit, instead of strawberries.

NUTRIENTS per serve

Energy	1462kJ
Energy	349cal
Total fat	8.2g
Saturated fat	4.3g
Monounsaturated fat	2.2g
Polyunsaturated fat	0.7g
Protein	15.0g
Carbohydrate	55.0g
Fibre	6.8g
Sodium	271mg
Cholesterol	26mg

TIP

Choose low or reduced fat dairy products (milk, cheese, yoghurt, ice-cream, custard) and calcium enriched soy products. Low or reduced fat dairy and soy products are suitable for the whole family, with the exception of children under the age of five who need full fat dairy or regular calcium enriched soy products to meet their high energy requirements.

Layered Fruit and Yoghurt with Bran

PREP TIME 10 minutes COOKING TIME Nil

1 cup bran flakes
400g reduced fat Greek style yoghurt or
    thick, reduced fat vanilla yoghurt
1/4 cup honey
2 peaches, stoned and sliced

200g strawberries, halved
1 kiwifruit, sliced
2 sugar bananas, sliced
1/2 cup sultanas

1 Divide the bran equally among four deep glasses. Top with yoghurt, then drizzle honey over the top.
2 Put the peaches, strawberries, kiwifruit and bananas in a bowl and gently mix to combine.
3 Spoon the fruit on top of the honey, then finish off with a generous sprinkle of sultanas. Serves 4

NUTRIENTS per serve

Energy	1385kJ
Energy	331cal
Total fat	2.2g
Saturated fat	1.1g
Monounsaturated fat	0.6g
Polyunsaturated fat	0.2g
Protein	9.3g
Carbohydrate	68.0g
Fibre	6.3g
Sodium	194mg
Cholesterol	10mg

Crunchy Wrapped Banana

PREP TIME 10 minutes COOKING TIME 5 minutes

4 sheets wholemeal lavash bread
200g reduced fat ricotta
2 tablespoons sunflower seeds
2 tablespoons sultanas

1 breakfast wheat biscuit, crushed
1 teaspoon ground cinnamon
2 tablespoons caster sugar
4 bananas, halved and sliced lengthwise

1 Lay the lavash out flat on a clean surface.
2 Put the ricotta, sunflower seeds, sultanas and wheat biscuit in a bowl and mix to combine.
3 Divide the ricotta mix among the lavash sheets and spread thick strips of the mixture along the centre of each.
4 Sprinkle with combined cinnamon and sugar mixture and top with banana. Roll up, put in a ridged sandwich press and toast until crisp and heated through. Serves 4

NUTRIENTS per serve

Energy	2291kJ
Energy	547cal
Total fat	11.0g
Saturated fat	3.5g
Monounsaturated fat	2.3g
Polyunsaturated fat	3.8g
Protein	20.0g
Carbohydrate	93.0g
Fibre	12.0g
Sodium	392mg
Cholesterol	21mg

Avocado, Spinach, Egg and Tomato Wrap

PREP TIME 10 minutes COOKING TIME 10 minutes

canola cooking spray
4 eggs
4 sheets wholemeal lavash bread
2 tablespoons reduced fat cream cheese

50g baby spinach leaves, washed
1 large avocado, sliced
2 vine ripened tomatoes, sliced
cracked black pepper to taste

1 Spray a non stick fry pan lightly with canola spray. Heat the pan, add the eggs and fry until done to your liking, remembering that they will cook further in the sandwich press.
2 While the eggs are cooking, lay the lavash out on a clean surface. Divide the cream cheese among the four pieces and spread along the centre.
3 Top with the spinach, avocado, tomato and egg and season with pepper.
4 Roll up, put in a ridged sandwich press and toast until crisp and heated through. Serves 4

NUTRIENTS per serve

Energy	1360kJ
Energy	325cal
Total fat	21.0g
Saturated fat	5.7g
Monounsaturated fat	11.0g
Polyunsaturated fat	2.6g
Protein	13.0g
Carbohydrate	21.0g
Fibre	5.7g
Sodium	349mg
Cholesterol	185mg

TIP
Both of these wraps are delicious served cold. If you do not have a sandwich press, try cooking them in a large non stick fry pan and weighing them down with a plate.

STAR INGREDIENT
LAVASH BREAD is a type of thin flatbread with a chewy texture. If the lavash has dried out, sprinkle it lightly with tepid water, wrap in a clean towel and allow to soften.

Crunchy Wrapped Banana (top) and Avocado, Spinach, Egg and Tomato Wrap (bottom)

NUTRIENTS per serve

Energy	558kJ
Energy	141cal
Total fat	6.8g
Saturated fat	3.5g
Monounsaturated fat	2.4g
Polyunsaturated fat	0.5g
Protein	6.9g
Carbohydrate	13.0g
Fibre	0.6g
Sodium	185mg
Cholesterol	17mg

STAR INGREDIENT
CANOLA PUFF PASTRY is made with canola oil rather than butter. It is high in monounsaturated fats whereas regular puff pastry (based on butter) is high in saturated fats. They both contain around the same amount of total fats, but the canola variety is more heart friendly.

NUTRIENTS per serve

Energy	955kJ
Energy	227cal
Total fat	5.9g
Saturated fat	1.0g
Monounsaturated fat	0.5g
Polyunsaturated fat	4.1g
Protein	5.0g
Carbohydrate	55.0g
Fibre	6.4g
Sodium	188mg
Cholesterol	30mg

Mini Thai Pork Sausage Rolls

PREP TIME 15 minutes COOKING TIME 20 minutes

500g lean pork mince
1 teaspoon ground cumin
1 teaspoon ground coriander
2 tablespoons sweet chilli sauce
2 tablespoons chopped fresh coriander

1 cup fresh breadcrumbs
4 sheets frozen canola puff pastry, thawed and halved lengthwise
2 tablespoons low or reduced fat milk

1 Preheat oven to 200°C.
2 Put the pork mince, cumin, ground coriander, sweet chilli sauce, fresh coriander and breadcrumbs in a bowl and mix to combine.
3 Spread one quarter of the mixture along one edge of one thawed sheet of pastry and roll up to conceal the filling. Repeat with the remaining filling and pastry sheets. Cut each roll into six bite size sausage rolls and place the rolls seam side down on two baking trays lined with non stick paper.
4 Lightly brush the rolls with milk and bake for 20 minutes or until the pastry is crisp and golden and the filling is cooked through.
5 Serve hot with tomato or sweet chilli sauce. Makes 24

Spiced Fruit Bread

PREP TIME 30 minutes COOKING TIME 1 hour

200g dried apricots, roughly chopped
200g dried figs, roughly chopped
200g pitted dried dates, roughly chopped
1 teaspoon bicarbonate of soda
2 cups self-raising flour, sifted

1 teaspoon ground ginger
1 teaspoon ground cinnamon
1/2 cup caster sugar
2 eggs, lightly beaten
2 tablespoons safflower oil

1 Preheat oven to 180°C. Grease and line a 24 x 12cm loaf tin with non stick baking paper.
2 Put the apricots, figs and dates in a medium pot, add 2 cups of water and bring to the boil. Reduce heat and simmer until nearly all the liquid has been absorbed. Stir in the bicarbonate of soda and allow to cool slightly.
3 Sift the flour and spices into a large bowl, stir in the sugar and make a well in the centre.
4 Add the combined eggs and oil and the cool fruit mixture. Spoon the mixture into the prepared tin and bake for 50 minutes or until a skewer inserted into the centre comes out clean.
5 Cool for 5 minutes in the tin before turning out onto a wire rack to cool completely. Makes 12 slices

NUTRIENTS per serve

Energy	1297kJ
Energy	310cal
Total fat	29.0g
Saturated fat	3.8g
Monounsaturated fat	19.0g
Polyunsaturated fat	4.8g
Protein	8.8g
Carbohydrate	4.5g
Fibre	3.6g
Sodium	229mg
Cholesterol	0mg

TIP

All nuts, with the exception of coconut, are brimming with polyunsaturated and monounsaturated fats. Eating a small handful of nuts several times a week is a heart healthy habit. However, if you are aiming to reduce your weight, go easy as they are quite high in kilojoules/calories.

NUTRIENTS per serve

Energy	555kJ
Energy	133cal
Total fat	8.0g
Saturated fat	3.3g
Monounsaturated fat	3.6g
Polyunsaturated fat	0.6g
Protein	10.0g
Carbohydrate	5.1g
Fibre	0.7g
Sodium	406mg
Cholesterol	68mg

TIP

Filo is a very thin pastry made from just flour and water. Unlike most other types of pastry it does not contain fats.

Chilli Soy Roasted Nuts

PREP TIME **5** minutes COOKING TIME **15** minutes

100g raw almonds
100g macadamias
100g unsalted cashews
100g unsalted raw peanuts

1 teaspoon five spice powder
1/4 teaspoon chilli powder
3 tablespoons reduced salt soy sauce
1 teaspoon sesame oil

1 Preheat oven to 180°C.
2 Put the almonds, macadamias, cashews and peanuts in a bowl and mix to combine. Add the five spice powder and chilli powder and toss the nuts in the spices.
3 Pour over the combined soy sauce and sesame oil and mix until all the nuts are coated.
4 Spread the nuts out on a non stick baking tray and bake for 15 minutes or until the nuts start to dry out and the soy coating darkens. Cool. Makes 2 cups. Serves 8

The nuts may be stored in an airtight container for up to a month.

Ham and Mushroom Filo Tartlets

PREP TIME **30** minutes COOKING TIME **30** minutes

canola cooking spray
1 tablespoon light olive oil
100g button mushrooms, sliced
6 spring onions, thinly sliced
1 clove garlic, crushed
50g reduced fat cheddar cheese, grated

200g reduced fat ricotta
2 eggs
1/2 teaspoon nutmeg
black pepper to taste
6 slices (125g) reduced fat ham
4 sheets of filo pastry

1 Preheat oven to 180°C. Spray 8 large (250 ml) muffin tins with canola spray.
2 Heat oil in a fry pan and cook the mushrooms, spring onions and garlic over a high heat for 3 minutes or until the mushrooms are browned. Cool slightly.
3 Put the mushrooms in a bowl, add the cheddar, ricotta, eggs and nutmeg and season with black pepper. Cut the ham into thin strips and fold into the mixture.
4 Lay the sheets of filo on top of each other, cut in half lengthwise then cut each even strip into four even pieces. Spray four pieces with cooking spray and layer unevenly in each muffin tin; repeat with three pieces.
5 Spoon the filling into the cases. Bake for 20-25 minutes until lightly golden. Leave for a few minutes before gently easing out and serve with a crisp green salad. Makes 8

Toasted Seed Risotto Balls

PREP TIME **30 minutes** + cooling and chilling   COOKING TIME **50 minutes**

1 litre reduced salt chicken or
   vegetable stock
2 teaspoons olive oil
3 spring onions, finely sliced
2 cloves garlic, crushed
275g arborio (risotto) rice

35g parmesan cheese, grated
50g reduced fat mozzarella cheese, grated
150g mixed salad seeds
   (eg sunflower and sesame)
olive oil cooking spray

1 Put the stock in a pot and bring to a gentle simmer. Heat the oil in a fry pan, add the spring onions and cook over a medium heat until golden. Add the garlic and rice and cook for a further 1-2 minutes, not allowing the rice to colour at all.
2 Add the stock ¹/2 cup at a time to the rice, stirring constantly until all the liquid is absorbed, then repeat until all the stock is used and the rice is cooked but still has a bite to it. Stir in the cheeses. Transfer the risotto to a bowl and leave to cool completely.
3 Using damp hands form the risotto mixture into 12 balls. Put the salad seeds in a food processor and process until they resemble rough breadcrumbs.
4 Spread the seeds on a plate and roll the balls in the seeds to cover completely. Place the balls on a paper-lined baking tray and chill for 10 minutes.
5 Preheat the oven to190°C. Lightly spray each ball with a little of the olive oil spray, place on a non stick baking tray and bake for 15-20 minutes until the outside is crisp and golden.
6 Serve with lemon wedges and green salad leaves on the side. Makes 12

These can be made into smaller balls and served as cocktail food.

NUTRIENTS per serve

Energy	787kJ
Energy	188cal
Total fat	9.4g
Saturated fat	1.9g
Monounsaturated fat	3.1g
Polyunsaturated fat	3.9g
Protein	6.9g
Carbohydrate	19.0g
Fibre	2.0g
Sodium	346mg
Cholesterol	5.98mg

TIP
In food labelling, 'cholesterol free' is not the same as 'fat free'. Many 'cholesterol free' foods still contain high levels of saturated fats and trans fats. If you suffer from high blood cholesterol, be sure to choose foods that are low in both saturated fats and trans fats.

STAR INGREDIENT
ARBORIO RICE is used to make risotto. The rice is first cooked in oil then simmering liquid (usually stock) is added very gradually. The rice slowly begins to swell and develops a wonderful creamy texture. Even after cooking, arborio rice should always retain a slight 'bite' in the centre which is called al dente or 'to the tooth'.

Iced Fruit Kebabs

| PREP TIME 20 minutes | COOKING TIME Nil |

1kg watermelon
200g strawberries

3 large mangoes
3 kiwifruit

1 Remove the rind and seeds from the watermelon, cut into 1.5cm thick slices and use a star cutter to cut shapes from the flesh. Cut the strawberries in half.
2 Cut the cheeks from the mango stone, remove the skin then cut each cheek into thick slices.
3 Remove the skin from the kiwifruit and cut into 1.5cm thick slices.
4 Thread the fruit onto bamboo skewers and place on a paper-lined non stick baking tray. Cover with plastic wrap and freeze until solid. Makes 8

NUTRIENTS per serve

Energy	333kJ
Energy	79cal
Total fat	0.5g
Saturated fat	0g
Monounsaturated fat	0g
Polyunsaturated fat	0g
Protein	1.8g
Carbohydrate	17.0g
Fibre	3.0g
Sodium	6.32mg
Cholesterol	0mg

TIP
Eating two of these delicious fruit kebabs is a great way to include the recommended two serves of fruit per day.

Hummus with Crisp Vegetables

| PREP TIME 30 minutes | COOKING TIME 5 minutes |

Hummus
400g can chickpeas
3 tablespoons lemon juice
2 cloves garlic, crushed
3 tablespoons tahini
1/4 teaspoon cumin

Vegetables and lavash
100g baby corn

1 carrot, cut into batons
1 red capsicum, cut into thick strips
1 sheet wholemeal lavash bread
olive oil cooking spray
1 clove garlic, crushed
1 tablespoon sesame seeds
20 baby spinach leaves, washed

1 Rinse the chickpeas and drain well. Put the chickpeas, lemon juice, 2 tablespoons water, garlic, tahini and cumin in a food processor and process until smooth. Transfer to a serving dish and prepare the vegetables.
2 Steam the baby corn until tender, rinse in cold water and drain well. Cut in half lengthwise.
3 Cut the lavash into large triangles and spray with olive oil spray. Top with garlic and sprinkle with sesame seeds. Grill until crisp and golden brown.
4 Arrange the vegetables around the hummus on a large serving platter. Makes 2 cups hummus. Serves 6

NUTRIENTS per serve

Energy	1240kJ
Energy	296cal
Total fat	9.4g
Saturated fat	1.2g
Monounsaturated fat	2.5g
Polyunsaturated fat	4.3g
Protein	16.0g
Carbohydrate	37.0g
Fibre	12.0g
Sodium	102mg
Cholesterol	0mg

TIP
Tahini is a paste made from ground sesame seeds. It provides polyunsaturated and monounsaturated fats and is ideal as a sandwich spread or with fresh salads and vegetables.

NUTRIENTS per serve

Energy	766kJ
Energy	183cal
Total fat	4.5g
Saturated fat	1.3g
Monounsaturated fat	1.5g
Polyunsaturated fat	0.8g
Protein	23.0g
Carbohydrate	12.0g
Fibre	5.0g
Sodium	574mg
Cholesterol	104mg

TIP

Skinless chicken breast fillets are generally the leanest cut of chicken, containing about 2.5g of fat per 100g compared to skinless leg or thigh which contains about 5.5g of fat per 100g.

NUTRIENTS per serve

Energy	1917kJ
Energy	458cal
Total fat	15.0g
Saturated fat	2.1g
Monounsaturated fat	5.5g
Polyunsaturated fat	3.8g
Protein	37.0g
Carbohydrate	45.0g
Fibre	4.6g
Sodium	632mg
Cholesterol	51mg

Tuna Niçoise

PREP TIME **20 minutes** COOKING TIME **20 minutes**

6 baby potatoes
1 red capsicum, chopped
2 medium vine ripened tomatoes, quartered
1 Lebanese cucumber, halved and sliced
400g canned artichokes, drained and quartered
100g kalamata olives
2 hard-boiled eggs, quartered
1/4 cup fresh basil leaves
2 x 200g cans tuna in lemon and pepper
125ml Italian salad dressing
1 tablespoon red wine vinegar
2 cloves garlic, crushed

1 Cook the potatoes in a large pot of boiling water until just tender, allow to cool then cut into quarters.
2 Put the potatoes, capsicum, tomatoes, cucumber, artichokes, olives, eggs and basil leaves in a large bowl and gently toss to combine.
3 Spoon the salad into individual bowls. Drain the tuna and break into large bite size pieces. Top the salad with tuna slices. Whisk the dressing, vinegar and garlic and drizzle over the salad. Serves 4-6

Hokkien Noodles with Lemon Grass Chicken

PREP TIME **15 minutes** COOKING TIME **15 minutes**

2 chicken breast fillets (about 400g)
1 stalk lemon grass, halved and bruised
400g hokkien noodles
2 spring onions, sliced
1 red capsicum, thinly sliced
1 carrot, thinly sliced
100g snow peas, halved
50g peanuts, toasted
2 tablespoons sesame seeds, toasted
2 tablespoons fresh Thai basil or mint leaves

Dressing
2 tablespoons sweet chilli sauce
1 tablespoon kecap manis (sweet soy sauce)
2 tablespoons lime juice
1 teaspoon peanut oil

1 Put the chicken breast fillets in a large deep fry pan with the lemon grass, just cover with water and bring to a simmer. Gently poach for 10-15 minutes or until tender. Allow to stand for 5 minutes then remove from the water and cut into thin slices. Finely chop the lemon grass and set aside to use in the dressing.
2 Gently separate the hokkien noodles and put in a large bowl. Cover with boiling water and allow to stand for 2 minutes then drain well.
3 Put the noodles, chicken, spring onions, capsicum, carrot, snow peas, peanuts, sesame seeds and basil leaves in a large bowl and prepare the dressing.
4 To make the dressing Put the chopped lemon grass, sweet chilli sauce, kecap manis, lime juice and peanut oil in a bowl and whisk to combine.
5 Pour the dressing over the other ingredients and toss gently. Serves 4

NUTRIENTS per serve	
Energy	1374kJ
Energy	328cal
Total fat	6.1g
Saturated fat	1.5g
Monounsaturated fat	1.7g
Polyunsaturated fat	2.2g
Protein	21.0g
Carbohydrate	47.0g
Fibre	9.0g
Sodium	799mg
Cholesterol	28mg

NUTRIENTS per serve	
Energy	1539kJ
Energy	368cal
Total fat	16g
Saturated fat	2.5g
Monounsaturated fat	4.0g
Polyunsaturated fat	8.4g
Protein	29.7g
Carbohydrate	26.0g
Fibre	4.8g
Sodium	824mg
Cholesterol	38mg

NUTRIENTS per serve	
Energy	2286kJ
Energy	546cal
Total fat	18.0g
Saturated fat	3.7g
Monounsaturated fat	9.3g
Polyunsaturated fat	3.1g
Protein	27.0g
Carbohydrate	70.0g
Fibre	6.0g
Sodium	1050mg
Cholesterol	31mg

Roast Beef and Horseradish on Rye

PREP TIME 10 minutes COOKING TIME Nil

8 thick slices rye bread
2 tablespoons horseradish cream
2 tablespoons polyunsaturated
  mayonnaise
2 tablespoons spicy tomato chutney

200g shaved rare roast beef
4 baby cos lettuce leaves
2 vine ripened tomatoes, cut into thick
  slices
black pepper to taste

1 Put the bread on a flat surface. Mix the horseradish cream, mayonnaise and tomato chutney together. Spread four of the rye slices with a little of the horseradish mixture.
2 Top with the rare roast beef, lettuce and tomatoes. Finish with a dollop of the horseradish mixture. Season with a little black pepper.
3 Place the remaining slices of rye bread on top and serve cut in half with a warm potato salad. Makes 4

Lemon Tuna and Butter Bean Baguettes

PREP TIME 10 minutes COOKING TIME Nil

4 small wholemeal baguettes
2 × 185g cans tuna in lemon and pepper
1 tablespoon polyunsaturated mayonnaise

1 tablespoon chopped fresh chives
300g can butter beans, drained
8 butter lettuce leaves

1 Cut a long deep pocket into each baguette.
2 Drain the tuna, reserving 2 tablespoons of the liquid. Add the mayonnaise and chopped chives to the liquid and whisk to combine. Put the tuna and butter beans in a bowl and gently mix to combine.
3 Tear the lettuce leaves into bite size pieces and place into the baguettes. Spoon in the tuna mixture then drizzle with the lemon pepper mayonnaise. Makes 4

Spicy Chicken and Beans in Lebanese Bread

PREP TIME 10 minutes COOKING TIME Nil

1 large avocado, chopped
2 teaspoons lemon juice
1/4 cup fresh coriander leaves
2 cups (245g) skinless barbecue chicken

1/2 cup bottled mild tomato salsa
4 wholemeal Lebanese bread rounds
1/4 cup canned spicy refried beans
cracked black pepper to taste

1 Put the avocado in a bowl, drizzle with the lemon juice then gently stir through the coriander. Shred the chicken (use white meat only) and combine with the salsa.
2 Lay the Lebanese bread out on a flat surface, divide the spicy refried beans among the rounds and spread evenly across the centre of each round.
3 Top with shredded chicken and chopped avocado, season with cracked black pepper and roll up firmly to enclose. Serve the rolls cut in half. Makes 4

Roast Beef (front right), Lemon Tuna (front left) and Spicy Chicken (back)

NUTRIENTS per serve

Energy	1386kJ
Energy	331cal
Total fat	17.0g
Saturated fat	2.7g
Monounsaturated fat	3.7g
Polyunsaturated fat	9.4g
Protein	18.0g
Carbohydrate	26.0g
Fibre	11.0g
Sodium	770mg
Cholesterol	30mg

TIP

Soy products such as soybeans, soybean oil, soy drinks and soy flour reduce blood cholesterol levels, especially when substituted for foods high in saturated fat.

Madras Curry Soy Burgers

PREP TIME **30 minutes** + chilling COOKING TIME **30 minutes**

2 tablespoons soybean oil
1 small onion, finely chopped
2 sticks celery, finely chopped
1 carrot, finely chopped
1 tablespoon Madras curry powder
2 × 420g cans soybeans
1 1/2 cups wholemeal breadcrumbs
2 tablespoons chopped fresh coriander

1 egg, lightly beaten
150g cherry tomatoes, quartered
3 spring onions, thinly sliced on the diagonal
black pepper to taste
6 hamburger buns or Turkish rolls
6 tablespoons hummus
6 butter lettuce leaves, washed

1 Heat 1 tablespoon of the oil in a large non stick fry pan, add the onion, celery and carrot and cook over a low heat for 5 minutes or until the vegetables are soft. Add the curry powder and cook for 2 minutes or until fragrant. Add 1 tablespoon of water to the pan if the curry powder starts to stick.
2 Drain the soybeans and rinse well. Put in a food processor with the vegetable mixture, breadcrumbs and 1 tablespoon of the coriander.
3 Process the mixture until well combined, add the egg and process for a few more seconds. Form the mixture into 6 patties and place on a paper-lined baking tray. Cover and chill for 30 minutes. Preheat the oven to 180°C.
4 Put the cherry tomatoes in a bowl, add the spring onions and the remaining coriander and mix to combine. Season with black pepper.
5 Heat a non stick fry pan, add the remaining oil then cook the soy burgers in batches until both sides are crisp and golden. Transfer them to the oven for 10 minutes to finish cooking.
6 Toast the buns and spread with the hummus, top the base of the buns with the lettuce, top with a burger, the tomato mixture and the top of the bun. Makes 6

NUTRIENTS per serve

Energy	1543kJ
Energy	369cal
Total fat	21.0g
Saturated fat	5.7g
Monounsaturated fat	11.0g
Polyunsaturated fat	3.1g
Protein	11.0g
Carbohydrate	33.0g
Fibre	11.0g
Sodium	503mg
Cholesterol	0.5mg

TIP

Brush avocado with a little lemon juice or vinegar to prevent it from turning brown.

Avocado and Bean Salad in Lettuce Baskets

PREP TIME **20 minutes** COOKING TIME **Nil**

130g can corn kernels, drained
300g can red kidney beans, rinsed and drained
1 small red onion, finely chopped
1 green capsicum, chopped
2 vine ripened tomatoes, chopped

1 large avocado, chopped
2 tablespoons mild bottled tomato salsa
2 tablespoons chopped fresh coriander
8 large iceberg lettuce leaves, washed
2 tablespoons reduced fat natural yoghurt
100g toasted corn chips

1 Put the corn, kidney beans, red onion, capsicum, tomatoes and avocado in a bowl and mix to combine.
2 Fold through the salsa and coriander. Spoon the salad into the lettuce leaves.
3 Top each lettuce cup with a dollop of yoghurt and a sprinkling of lightly crushed corn chips. Serves 4

This salad also makes a delicious filling for burritos, wraps or tacos.

Baked Pasta with Turkey and Cranberry

PREP TIME **20 minutes** COOKING TIME **30 minutes**

canola cooking spray
200g farfalle (butterfly or bow tie pasta)
100g baby spinach leaves, washed
200g light turkey breast, shaved

6 eggs, lightly beaten
125ml low or reduced fat milk
$^1/_3$ cup grated reduced fat cheddar cheese
2 tablespoons cranberry sauce

1 Preheat oven to 180°C. Spray 6 large (250 ml) muffin tins with canola spray and line the bases with baking paper.
2 Cook the farfalle in a large pot of rapidly boiling water until just tender; drain well.
3 Line the bases and sides of the muffin tins with the farfalle. Steam the spinach until it wilts, drain well and squeeze out any excess moisture.
4 Fill the centre of each muffin tin with turkey breast and spinach.
5 Whisk together the eggs, milk and cheese and pour into the muffin tins. Top with a spoonful of cranberry sauce. Bake for 20 minutes or until set. Turn out and serve with a green salad. Makes 6

NUTRIENTS per serve

Energy	1035kJ
Energy	247cal
Total fat	7.6g
Saturated fat	2.6g
Monounsaturated fat	2.7g
Polyunsaturated fat	1.0g
Protein	20.0g
Carbohydrate	25.0g
Fibre	2.1g
Sodium	195mg
Cholesterol	199mg

TIP

For a cheese to be labelled 'reduced fat', it must not contain more than 75% of the total fat content of the regular full fat variety. Regular cheddar cheese contains around 34g fat per 100g so reduced fat cheddar must be reduced in fat by at least 25% (a maximum of 25g fat per 100g). Reduced fat cheese still contains a fair amount of total and saturated fats, so use small quantities only.

STAR INGREDIENT

FARFALLE means butterfly in Italian and refers to the delicate shape of this dry pasta. It is also sometimes called bow, or bow tie, pasta. Farfalle is rich in carbohydrates, contains some protein and dietary fibre, and small quantities of vitamins and minerals.

Mini Beef and Pine Nut Meatloaves

PREP TIME 15 minutes	COOKING TIME 30 minutes

canola cooking spray
480g lean beef mince
1 small onion, finely grated
1 small carrot, finely grated
2 tablespoons pine nuts, toasted

1 teaspoon mixed dried herbs
1 egg, lightly beaten
1 cup fresh breadcrumbs
2 tablespoons reduced salt tomato sauce

1 Preheat oven to 180°C. Spray 4 large (250 ml) muffin tins with canola spray.
2 Put the mince, onion, carrot, pine nuts, herbs, egg and breadcrumbs in a bowl and mix to combine.
3 Divide mixture among the four greased muffin tins and press in firmly. Spread the tops with the tomato sauce and bake for 30 minutes or until cooked through. Each meatloaf will start to come away from the edges of its tin when cooked.
4 Serve hot or cold with wholegrain bread and salad. Serves 4

STAR INGREDIENT
LEMONS and other citrus fruit are high in vitamin C and contain flavonoids which act as antioxidants in the body. Lemons and limes add wonderful flavour to dishes and are a great alternative to salty cooking sauces.

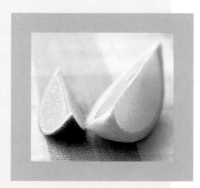

Salmon and Creamed Corn Patties

PREP TIME 20 minutes + chilling	COOKING TIME 25 minutes

3 potatoes (about 400g), peeled and chopped
100g dry rice vermicelli
420g canned, no added salt red salmon, drained
2 egg whites, lightly beaten
130g can creamed corn

4 spring onions, sliced
1 red capsicum, finely chopped
2 cups fresh breadcrumbs
2 tablespoons chopped fresh dill
1-2 tablespoons lemon juice
olive oil cooking spray

1 Cook the potatoes in a large pot of water until soft. Drain, return to the pot and cook over a low heat until dry. Remove from the heat and mash until smooth.
2 Put the vermicelli in a large bowl, cover with boiling water and set aside for 10 minutes or until soft. Drain well and cut into short pieces using kitchen scissors.
3 Put the potatoes, vermicelli, salmon, egg whites, corn, spring onions, capsicum, breadcrumbs, dill and lemon juice in a bowl and combine well.
4 Divide the mixture into eight and shape each portion into a flat patty. Put on a baking tray lined with non stick baking paper and refrigerate for 30 minutes or until firm. Preheat the oven to 200°C.
5 Lightly spray a non stick fry pan with olive oil spray and heat over a medium heat until hot. Cook the patties in batches until golden brown on both sides, transfer to the oven and cook for 10-15 minutes more or until heated through. Makes 8

This recipe can also be made using canned tuna or crab in place of the salmon.

A guide to shopping for healthier food choices

Choosing food products that are healthier for your heart doesn't have to be hard work. Here's what you need to know.

The Heart Foundation's Tick Food Information Program is a simple guide to making healthier food choices quickly and easily. The Tick logo identifies healthy food choices within the food categories. There are now over 1200 foods approved to display the Tick. All of these products must meet the Heart Foundation's strict nutritional guidelines for fat, saturated fat, sodium (salt), dietary fibre and added sugar.

For a food product to get a Tick it must be tested independently of the manufacturer. Manufacturers work hard to achieve the Tick guidelines and many products have been modified to meet them.

The Heart Foundation's Tick Nutrition Team works closely with food manufacturers to ensure correct nutrition information is displayed on their food packaging, and to help them comply with food labelling laws. This means that shoppers can trust the program and confidently pick the Tick.

FOOD LABELS - Making it simple

Food labels are a useful guide when purchasing nutritious foods
◆ The ingredient list indicates the major ingredients the food contains.
◆ The nutrition information panel lists the key nutritional attributes of the food (see table 1 at right).

How to read the ingredient list
◆ Ingredients are listed in order from the largest to the smallest amount used, based on the weight of the ingredient.
◆ The major ingredients in a food product are usually listed in the first three ingredients. For instance, if the second

ingredient is animal fat, the product will most probably be high in saturated fat.

What to look out for in the ingredient list
◆ If several high saturated fat ingredients are listed in the food product, the overall saturated fat content of the product will also be high.
◆ High saturated fat ingredients include animal fat, hydrogenated fat, tallow, butter, palm oil (often simply called vegetable oil or fat), shortening, ghee, lard, dripping, coconut oil, coconut cream, copha, full cream milk solids, mono- or diglycerides.

Per serving size
This column indicates the nutritional content of a single serving of the food product as recommended by the manufacturer. This may not correspond to your actual serving size. For different serving sizes, you will need to adapt the nutritional information accordingly.

Per 100g
This column indicates the nutritional content of 100g of the food product. This is useful for comparing the nutritional content of 100g of similar food products. For instance, you can use it to compare the saturated fat content of different types of dips to select the one lowest in saturated fat.

◆ **Energy** is the amount of kilojoules or calories in the food product. If you are managing your body weight, consider the amount of kilojoules or calories in food products that you eat frequently.

◆ **Fat, total** is the total amount of fat in the food product. It includes the amount of fat from the three main types of fat: saturated, polyunsaturated and monounsaturated.

◆ **Saturated fat** increases the risk of heart disease. Look for food products low in saturated fat.

◆ **Carbohydrate, total** is the total amount of carbohydrate in the food product from starches, naturally occurring sugars and added sugars.

◆ **Carbohydrate, sugars** includes sugars found naturally in foods (such as lactose in milk, or fructose in fruit) as well as added sugar (such as table sugar). The nutrition information panel does not highlight the source of sugar in the product. Use the ingredient list to find out the source of sugar in the food product. If sugar or similar ingredients (eg dextrose, fructose, honey) appear in the first three ingredients, you will know that the food product is high in added sugar. However, if dried fruit features in the first three ingredients, then the added sugar is more likely to be naturally occurring. Sugar does not increase the risk of heart disease or diabetes. It does provide unnecessary calories if you are trying to restrict your energy intake.

◆ **Sodium (salt)** content can be checked by using the 'per 100g' column to compare the sodium content of similar food products. Use the 'per serving' column to find out how much sodium will be consumed in each serve.

NUTRITION CLAIMS - What do they really mean?

◆ **Cholesterol free** simply means that the food product is free of cholesterol. It does not necessarily mean that the food is low in saturated fat, or that it will help lower the amount of cholesterol in your blood.

◆ **Low fat** means the food must contain 3 percent or less fat (if solid) or

1.5 percent or less fat (if liquid). Foods making a low fat claim must feature a nutrition information panel.

◆ **Reduced fat** products have 25 percent less fat than the regular food product. They are not necessarily low fat products.

◆ **Light or lite** can mean less fat or salt. It can also mean light in flavour, as in the case of 'lite' olive oil. Check the nutrition label to find out the difference between the light food product and the regular food product.

◆ **Low salt** means the food product contains no more than 120mg of sodium per 100g.

◆ **Reduced salt** means the food product has 25 percent less sodium than the regular food product.

Beside every recipe in this book you'll find an analysis of the nutrients per serve. This includes an analysis of the total fat and type of fat in each recipe, as well as other important nutrients (see page 154).

Heart Foundation

For further information on any heart health issue, ring the Heart Foundation's **HEARTLINE** on 1300 36 27 87 (for the cost of a local call).

TABLE 1: How to read the nutrition information panel
Example - a 98% Fat Free Dip Servings per package: 11 Serving size: 20g

	Per 20g serving	Per 100g
Energy	119kJ	595kJ
Protein	1.5g	7.7g
Fat, total	0.3g	1.7g
- saturated fat	Nil	Nil
Carbohydrate		
- total	3.1g	15.3g
- sugars	1.6g	8.2g
Sodium	25mg	123mg
Potassium	76mg	382mg

Soups and Starters

Delicious, nutritious soups and starters: they taste great, provide plenty of goodness, and keep you on the right track for a healthy lifestyle. Discover the pleasures of a leisurely start to a grand meal with friends, or stock up for solo meals with our best soup and starter suggestions.

Rustic Mediterranean Seafood Soup

PREP TIME **25 minutes** COOKING TIME **25 minutes**

200g calamari tubes, cleaned
300g green prawns
200g mussels
250g mixed firm white fish fillets
   (red mullet, sea perch, red fish)
1 tablespoon olive oil
2 cloves garlic, crushed

1 onion, finely chopped
125ml white wine
400g can chopped tomatoes
750ml reduced salt fish stock
pinch saffron
2 potatoes (about 300g), peeled and cut
   into large cubes

1 Cut the calamari tubes into rings. Peel and devein the prawns, leaving the tails intact. Scrub the mussels and remove the hairy beards. Discard any that are already open. Remove any bones from the fish and cut into large pieces.
2 Heat the oil in a large pot. Add the garlic and onion and cook over a medium heat for 3 minutes or until the onion is golden. Add the white wine and bring to the boil. Cook over a high heat until nearly all the liquid has been absorbed.
3 Add the tomatoes, fish stock, saffron and potatoes and simmer for 15 minutes or until the potatoes are tender. Do not overcook or they will start to break up.
4 Add all the seafood and simmer for 3-5 minutes or until tender. Serve with crusty Italian bread. Serves 6

Try fresh clams instead of mussels, or use a combination of the two.

Sweet Potato, Pasta and Leek Soup

PREP TIME **20 minutes** COOKING TIME **40 minutes**

2 teaspoons canola oil
2 leeks, thinly sliced
pinch saffron
1kg orange sweet potato, peeled and
   chopped
1 litre reduced salt chicken stock
1 cinnamon stick
1 bouquet garni (flavouring herbs)

100g ditalini (tiny pasta pieces for soup)
2 tablespoons chopped fresh chives

Lavash crisps
2 sheets lavash bread
1 tablespoon olive oil
2 tablespoons finely grated parmesan
   cheese

1 Heat the oil in a large pot, add the leeks and cook over a medium heat for 5 minutes or until the leeks are soft and golden. Add the saffron and sweet potato and stir for about 5 minutes or until the sweet potato begins to soften.
2 Stir in the stock, cinnamon stick and bouquet garni. Bring to the boil then reduce the heat and simmer for 30 minutes or until the sweet potato is very soft. Remove the cinnamon stick and bouquet garni.
3 Cook the pasta in a large pot of rapidly boiling water until al dente (cooked, but still with a bite to it). Drain well.
4 Puree the soup in batches until smooth then return to the pot along with the pasta and reheat gently. If it is too thick add a little water.
5 To make lavash crisps Use a star-shaped cookie cutter to cut out shapes from the bread, brush lightly with oil, sprinkle with parmesan and place another star on top. Grill until crisp and golden.
6 To serve, ladle the soup into bowls, float lavash stars on top and sprinkle with chives. Serves 6

NUTRIENTS per serve

Energy	8741kJ
Energy	209cal
Total fat	5.3g
Saturated fat	1.1g
Monounsaturated fat	2.8g
Polyunsaturated fat	0.7g
Protein	27.0g
Carbohydrate	9.8g
Fibre	2.1g
Sodium	537mg
Cholesterol	170mg

TIP
Non-oily fish can be kept frozen for up to 4-6 months and oily fish can be frozen for 3 months. Whole fish should be gilled and gutted before freezing. Wrap each whole fish, fillet or cutlet in plastic with a dated label before freezing. When the fish is frozen solid, dip it in cold water and return it to the freezer to form a protective ice glaze.

NUTRIENTS per serve

Energy	1442kJ
Energy	344cal
Total fat	6.8g
Saturated fat	1.4g
Monounsaturated fat	3.3g
Polyunsaturated fat	1.1g
Protein	9.9g
Carbohydrate	61.0g
Fibre	5.9g
Sodium	818mg
Cholesterol	3mg

Minted Pea and Potato Soup

PREP TIME 10 minutes	COOKING TIME 25 minutes

4 potatoes (about 500g), peeled and chopped
1 litre reduced salt chicken stock
1 bay leaf

450g frozen baby mint peas
2 large sprigs basil
4 tablespoons reduced fat sour cream
cracked black pepper to taste

1 Put the potatoes and stock in a large pot and bring to the boil. Add the bay leaf and simmer over a medium heat for 15 minutes or until the potatoes are just tender.
2 Add the peas and basil and simmer for 5 minutes or until the peas are tender, taking care not to overcook or the peas will lose their rich colour. Remove the bay leaf and basil and discard.
3 Process the soup in batches until smooth, then return to the pot and reheat gently.
4 Ladle the soup into bowls and put a spoonful of sour cream into the centre of each. Stir gently with a skewer to make a swirl pattern in the top of the soup and season with cracked black pepper. Serves 6

NUTRIENTS per serve

Energy	534kJ
Energy	128cal
Total fat	3.3g
Saturated fat	1.8g
Monounsaturated fat	0.7g
Polyunsaturated fat	0.1g
Protein	7.0g
Carbohydrate	17.0g
Fibre	5.7g
Sodium	565mg
Cholesterol	8.96mg

STAR INGREDIENT

POTATOES are often accused of being fattening. But they are fat free and a great source of carbohydrate. Potatoes are a good source of vitamin C and also provide dietary fibre, potassium, thiamin and niacin.

Pumpkin Damper

PREP TIME 15 minutes	COOKING TIME 40 minutes

2 1/2 cups self-raising flour
1 teaspoon baking powder
1 cup mashed pumpkin
1 tablespoon chopped fresh lemon thyme

1 egg, lightly beaten
1 tablespoon low or reduced fat milk
2 tablespoons sunflower seeds

1 Preheat oven to 180°C. Sift the flour and baking powder into a large bowl, make a well in the centre and stir in the pumpkin and thyme.
2 Whisk together the egg and milk and stir into the mixture with a flat bladed knife until a soft dough forms.
3 Turn out onto a lightly floured surface and knead until smooth. Shape into a large ball and flatten slightly.
4 Place onto a non stick baking tray and use a sharp knife to cut the damper into eight equal portions, but do not separate the pieces.
5 Brush the damper with water and sprinkle with sunflower seeds. Bake for 40 minutes or until cooked. It will sound hollow when tapped.
6 Allow to cool slightly before cutting. Serves 8

You will need about 400g of raw pumpkin to make 1 cup mashed.

NUTRIENTS per serve

Energy	776kJ
Energy	185cal
Total fat	2.9g
Saturated fat	0.5g
Monounsaturated fat	0.6g
Polyunsaturated fat	1.4g
Protein	6.5g
Carbohydrate	33.0g
Fibre	2.4g
Sodium	313mg
Cholesterol	23mg

Thai Prawn Soup with Lemon Grass

| PREP TIME 20 minutes | COOKING TIME 20 minutes |

500g large green prawns
3 stalks lemon grass
1 litre reduced salt fish stock
2cm piece ginger, peeled and cut into fine strips
2 kaffir lime leaves, finely shredded
1/2 small pineapple, peeled and cored

1/2 tablespoon fish sauce
1 tablespoon lime juice
6 spring onions, thinly sliced on the diagonal
1/2 cup fresh coriander leaves
pepper to taste

1 Peel and devein the prawns, leaving the tails intact. Reserve the shells and discard the veins. Halve the lemon grass stalks and squash the bases with the flat side of a knife.
2 Place the prawn shells in a medium pot with the stock and bring slowly to the boil. Reduce the heat and simmer gently for 10 minutes. Strain, return to the pot and add the lemon grass, ginger and lime leaves and return to simmering point.
3 Cut the pineapple into thin pieces and add to the stock along with the prawns and simmer just until the prawns turn pink and tender (a few minutes, depending on their size). Add the fish sauce, lime juice, spring onions and coriander.
4 Remove the lemon grass and lime leaves, season with pepper and serve immediately. Serves 6

NUTRIENTS per serve

Energy	464kJ
Energy	110cal
Total fat	0.8g
Saturated fat	0.1g
Monounsaturated fat	0.1g
Polyunsaturated fat	0.1g
Protein	19.0g
Carbohydrate	7.1g
Fibre	1.9g
Sodium	848mg
Cholesterol	124mg

TIP

If possible, use the paper bags provided in supermarkets when buying mushrooms. Mushrooms tend to sweat in plastic bags and will perish quickly.

Mixed Mushroom Noodle Soup

| PREP TIME 15 minutes + standing | COOKING TIME 20 minutes |

8 (30g) dried shiitake mushrooms
1 litre reduced salt vegetable stock
3cm piece ginger, crushed
1 halved garlic clove
1 whole star anise
1 tablespoon reduced salt soy sauce

100g oyster mushrooms
400g fresh udon noodles
3 spring onions, sliced
100g enoki mushrooms, gently separated

1 Put the shiitake mushrooms in an ovenproof bowl, add 1 cup boiling water and allow to stand for 25 minutes or until the mushrooms are soft. Drain, then strain and reserve the liquid. Cut the mushrooms into thin slices.
2 Put the stock, mushroom liquid, ginger, garlic, star anise and soy into a large pot and bring to the boil. Reduce the heat and simmer for 10 minutes. Remove the ginger, garlic and star anise and discard.
3 Add the oyster mushrooms, dried shiitake, udon noodles and spring onions and simmer gently for 5 minutes.
4 Stir in the enoki and heat for 1 minute or until they soften. Serve hot. Serves 6

NUTRIENTS per serve

Energy	1056kJ
Energy	252cal
Total fat	1.3g
Saturated fat	0g
Monounsaturated fat	0g
Polyunsaturated fat	0g
Protein	10.6g
Carbohydrate	48.6g
Fibre	2.9g
Sodium	670mg
Cholesterol	12mg

Curried Broccoli and Split Pea Soup with Garlic Naan

PREP TIME **15 minutes**   COOKING TIME **1 hour 15 minutes**

2 teaspoons corn oil
1 onion, sliced
1 tablespoon Madras curry paste
1 cup yellow split peas
1/2 cup brown lentils
1 litre reduced salt vegetable stock
500g English spinach, washed and
   chopped

300g broccoli, cut into florets
1 tablespoon lemon juice

Garlic naan (Indian bread)
2 plain naan or pita rounds
2 cloves garlic, crushed
1 tablespoon corn oil
1 teaspoon cumin seeds

1 Heat the oil in a large pot, add the onion and curry paste and cook for a few minutes until the onion is soft and the curry paste is fragrant.

2 Add the split peas, lentils, vegetable stock and 500ml water and bring to the boil, skimming occasionally to remove any scum. Cover and simmer for 1 hour or until both the peas and lentils are quite soft.

3 Add the chopped spinach and broccoli and simmer for a couple of minutes until the broccoli is tender. Season with lemon juice.

4 To make the garlic naan   Preheat oven to 180°C. Put the naan onto two non stick baking trays, brush with the combined garlic and oil, then sprinkle with cumin seeds. Wrap in foil and bake for 15 minutes or until warmed through. Cut into thick strips and serve hot with the soup. Serves 6

NUTRIENTS per serve

Energy	1743kJ
Energy	416cal
Total fat	8.4g
Saturated fat	1.1g
Monounsaturated fat	1.7g
Polyunsaturated fat	4.2g
Protein	23.0g
Carbohydrate	62.0g
Fibre	12.0g
Sodium	988mg
Cholesterol	0.3mg

STAR INGREDIENT
BROCCOLI is closely related to cauliflower and among the most nutritious vegetables available. It is an excellent source of vitamin C and a good source of dietary fibre and potassium. It also contains carotene, vitamin E and several B group vitamins, including folate.

TIP
You can easily reduce the overall salt content of recipes by choosing a reduced salt stock. To reduce further the salt content of soups and other meals requiring stock, simply substitute part of the volume of stock required with water.

Chicken Vegetable Soup with Cheese Sticks

PREP TIME **30 minutes** COOKING TIME **40 minutes**

2 skinless chicken breast fillets
1 litre reduced salt chicken stock
1 tablespoon canola oil
2 leeks, washed and thinly sliced
2 carrots, diced
2 sticks celery, diced
3 cloves garlic, crushed
6 cups young green leaves (watercress,
    rocket, sorrel, baby spinach), washed

3 tablespoons fresh pesto (see page 62)
cracked black pepper to taste

Cheese sticks
1 sheet canola puff pastry, thawed
3 tablespoons finely grated reduced fat
    cheese

1 Put the chicken in a pot, add just enough chicken stock to cover and poach gently for about 10 minutes or until just cooked. Set aside to cool.
2 Heat the oil in a large pot, add the leeks and cook gently for about 2 minutes until soft. Add the carrot, celery and garlic, strain the chicken poaching stock through a fine sieve and add to the vegetables with the rest of the stock. Simmer for 10 minutes. Chop the greens finely, add to the soup and cook for a further 10 minutes.
3 Tear the chicken breasts into fine shreds and add them to the soup. Stir in the pesto and season with plenty of cracked black pepper.
4 To make cheese sticks Preheat oven to 220°C. Cut the puff pastry into 2cm thick strips and place on a paper lined baking tray. Sprinkle with the cheese and bake for 20 minutes or until crisp and golden.
5 Serve the soup in wide bowls with cheese sticks. Serves 6

Spiced Fish, Tomato and Chickpea Soup

PREP TIME 15 minutes + standing COOKING TIME **35 minutes**

1 tablespoon olive oil
1 onion, chopped
1 teaspoon ground coriander
1 teaspoon ground cumin
1 teaspoon allspice
1 green chilli, finely sliced
400g can chopped tomatoes
400g can chickpeas, rinsed and drained
1 litre reduced salt fish stock

500g firm white fish fillets (redfish, bream,
    sea perch), cut into large pieces
1/3 cup couscous
thick, reduced fat natural yoghurt, to serve
1 tablespoon chopped fresh parsley
1 tablespoon chopped fresh mint
Lebanese bread, to serve

1 Heat the oil in a large pot, add the onion and cook over a medium heat for 3 minutes or until the onion is soft and golden.
2 Add the spices and chilli and cook until fragrant, about 2 minutes. Stir in the tomatoes, chickpeas and fish stock and bring to the boil. Reduce the heat and simmer uncovered for 15 minutes.
3 Add the fish and cook for 5 minutes or just until the fish is tender. Remove the soup from the heat then add the couscous and cover. Set aside for 10 minutes or until the couscous is soft.
4 Serve with a dollop of yoghurt and sprinkled with parsley and mint. Accompany with wedges of Lebanese bread. Serves 6

NUTRIENTS per serve
Energy	1781kJ
Energy	426cal
Total fat	22g
Saturated fat	8.5g
Monounsaturated fat	8.7g
Polyunsaturated fat	2.3g
Protein	37.0g
Carbohydrate	21.0g
Fibre	4.9g
Sodium	1227mg
Cholesterol	81mg

STAR INGREDIENT
CHILLIES are all hot but the smallest ones are the hottest, and even more so when green. Discard chilli seeds to reduce their heat in a dish, and wash your hands immediately after handling them as their oils can irritate the skin. If fresh chillies are not available, use flakes or powdered chilli.

NUTRIENTS per serve
Energy	1450kJ
Energy	346cal
Total fat	9.9g
Saturated fat	1.9g
Monounsaturated fat	3.6g
Polyunsaturated fat	2.7g
Protein	31.0g
Carbohydrate	33.0g
Fibre	10.0g
Sodium	687mg
Cholesterol	58mg

Lemon Grass Beef Parcels

PREP TIME 15 minutes + standing COOKING TIME 10 minutes

NUTRIENTS per serve

Energy	213kJ
Energy	51cal
Total fat	1.4g
Saturated fat	0.5g
Monounsaturated fat	0.5g
Polyunsaturated fat	0.1g
Protein	6.7g
Carbohydrate	2.7g
Fibre	0.7g
Sodium	142mg
Cholesterol	20mg

50g Chinese (mung bean) vermicelli
350g lean beef mince
1/2 cup bean sprouts
2 stalks lemon grass, finely chopped
1 tablespoon lemon juice
1 tablespoon fish sauce

2 spring onions, thinly sliced
200g can water chestnuts,
   drained and finely chopped
12 rice paper wrappers
12 fresh mint leaves
sweet chilli sauce, for dipping

1 Put the vermicelli in a bowl, cover with boiling water and allow to stand for 10 minutes or until soft. Drain well.
2 Put the beef mince and 3 tablespoons of water in a fry pan and cook over a high heat for about 10 minutes or until the beef is tender and cooked. Drain off any excess liquid.
3 Transfer the beef to a bowl, add the bean sprouts, lemon grass, lemon juice, fish sauce, spring onions and water chestnuts.
4 Soak the rice paper wrappers one at a time in a bowl of warm water until soft or allow each guest a bowl of water and let them soak their own.
5 Place a mint leaf at the end of a wrapper, place 2 tablespoons of the beef mixture on the wrapper, fold in the ends and roll up to enclose.
6 Serve with sweet chilli sauce. Makes 12

TIP
The recipe for Lemon Grass Beef Parcels is also delicious made with lean chicken or pork mince instead of beef. If you do not have rice paper wrappers use lettuce or English spinach leaves instead.

STAR INGREDIENT
LEMON GRASS is a fragrant, tropical grass and should have its tough outer stems removed before use. Generally, only the white part is used but the whole stem can be used in curries if it is removed before serving. The stem can be bruised (to release its aroma), finely sliced or chopped.

NUTRIENTS per serve

Energy	549kJ
Energy	131cal
Total fat	3.0g
Saturated fat	0.7g
Monounsaturated fat	0.7g
Polyunsaturated fat	1.0g
Protein	17.0g
Carbohydrate	8.6g
Fibre	3.1g
Sodium	807mg
Cholesterol	179mg

STAR INGREDIENT

SCALLOPS are a good source of protein and zinc. They contain very little fat. Scallops need only a minute or two to cook as overcooking will cause them to toughen and spoil their sweet, tender flesh.

NUTRIENTS per serve

Energy	873kJ
Energy	209cal
Total fat	5.6g
Saturated fat	0.8g
Monounsaturated fat	3.6g
Polyunsaturated fat	0.6g
Protein	10.0g
Carbohydrate	19.0g
Fibre	2.7g
Sodium	105mg
Cholesterol	17mg

Chargrilled Baby Octopus Salad

PREP TIME **20 minutes** + marinating COOKING TIME **10 minutes**

360g cleaned baby octopus
1 teaspoon sesame oil
1 tablespoon lime juice
1/4 cup sweet chilli sauce
1 tablespoon fish sauce
50g rice vermicelli

100g mixed salad leaves
1 cup bean sprouts
1 Lebanese cucumber, halved
200g cherry tomatoes, halved
1/2 cup fresh coriander sprigs
lime wedges, to serve

1 Rinse the cleaned octopus and pat dry with paper towel.
2 Put the sesame oil, lime juice, sweet chilli sauce and fish sauce in a jug and whisk to combine. Pour over the octopus and coat the octopus in the marinade. Cover with plastic wrap and marinate for 4 hours or overnight. Drain and reserve the marinade.
3 Put the vermicelli in a bowl, cover with boiling water and allow to stand for 10 minutes or until soft. Drain well.
4 Divide the mixed salad leaves among four plates, top with the bean sprouts, rice vermicelli, cucumber and tomato.
5 Cook the octopus on a preheated chargrill or barbecue until tender and well coloured. Put the marinade in a small pot and bring to the boil. Serve the octopus on top of the salad, drizzle with the hot marinade and garnish with coriander and lime wedges. Serves 4

Asparagus with Seared Scallops and White Wine Dressing

PREP TIME **10 minutes** COOKING TIME **20 minutes**

4 kipfler potatoes, peeled
2 bunches asparagus, trimmed
olive oil cooking spray
16 scallops without roe
2 cloves garlic, crushed
1 tablespoon lemon zest

250ml dry white wine
2 tablespoons lemon juice
1 teaspoon white sugar
20g olive oil spread
cracked black pepper to taste
fresh chervil leaves, to serve

1 Steam or microwave the potatoes until tender. Drain and allow to cool slightly before cutting into thick slices.
2 Steam or microwave the asparagus until tender; drain well.
3 Spray a non stick fry pan with olive oil spray and heat. Cook the scallops in batches over a high heat just until they are golden, about a minute on each side. Remove from the pan and keep warm. Do not overcook or they will be tough.
4 Add the garlic, lemon zest, white wine, lemon juice and sugar to the pan and bring to the boil. Stir and then simmer until reduced by half.
5 Stir in the olive oil spread and cook until it melts. Season with cracked black pepper.
6 Divide the asparagus among four serving plates, top with sliced potato and scallops and drizzle with white wine dressing. Garnish with the fresh chervil leaves and serve immediately. Serves 4

Tomato, Garlic and Basil Bruschetta

NUTRIENTS per serve	
Energy	565kJ
Energy	135cal
Total fat	1.4g
Saturated fat	0.4g
Monounsaturated fat	0.3g
Polyunsaturated fat	0.4g
Protein	5.3g
Carbohydrate	25.0g
Fibre	2.2g
Sodium	352mg
Cholesterol	0mg

PREP TIME 10 minutes COOKING TIME 5 minutes

1 loaf ciabatta or 1 French stick
2 cloves garlic, halved

Tomato, garlic and basil
2 vine ripened tomatoes, chopped

1 clove garlic, crushed
1 tablespoon basil, finely shredded
cracked black pepper

1 To make the bruschetta base Cut the bread into thick slices and toast both sides until crisp and golden. Rub one side of each bread slice with the garlic.
2 To make the tomato, garlic and basil topping Combine the chopped tomato, garlic and shredded basil. Spoon on top of the toasts and sprinkle with cracked black pepper. Makes 8

Sardine and Ricotta Bruschetta

NUTRIENTS per serve	
Energy	907kJ
Energy	217cal
Total fat	7.3g
Saturated fat	2.7g
Monounsaturated fat	2.2g
Polyunsaturated fat	1.9g
Protein	13.0g
Carbohydrate	25.0g
Fibre	1.7g
Sodium	564mg
Cholesterol	41mg

PREP TIME 10 minutes COOKING TIME 5 minutes

1 loaf ciabatta or 1 French stick
2 cloves garlic, halved

Ricotta and sardine
100g reduced fat ricotta cheese

zest of 1 lemon
1 tablespoon fresh thyme, chopped
2 × 125g cans sardines, drained, halved,
    and bones removed
1/2 lemon, very thinly sliced

1 To make the bruschetta base Cut the bread into thick slices and toast both sides until crisp and golden. Rub one side of each bread slice with the garlic.
2 To make the ricotta and sardine topping Put the ricotta, lemon zest and thyme in a bowl and mix to combine. Spread the ricotta over the toasts and top with sardines and lemon slices. Makes 8

Capsicum and Caper Bruschetta

NUTRIENTS per serve	
Energy	722kJ
Energy	173cal
Total fat	5.0g
Saturated fat	1.2g
Monounsaturated fat	2.0g
Polyunsaturated fat	1.5g
Protein	6.0g
Carbohydrate	25.0g
Fibre	2.1g
Sodium	361mg
Cholesterol	2.42mg

PREP TIME 10 minutes COOKING TIME 10 minutes

1 loaf ciabatta or 1 French stick
2 cloves garlic, halved

Capsicum and caper
1 yellow capsicum, seeded
1 red capsicum, seeded

1 tablespoon pine nuts, toasted
1 tablespoon baby capers
1 tablespoon balsamic vinegar
2 teaspoons extra virgin olive oil
2 tablespoons reduced fat cream cheese

1 To make the bruschetta base Cut the bread into thick slices and toast both sides until crisp and golden. Rub one side of each bread slice with the garlic.
2 To make the capsicum and caper topping Cut the yellow and red capsicum into large flat pieces and cook skin side up under a preheated grill on high for a couple of minutes or until the skin blisters and blackens. Put in a plastic bag and allow to cool. Peel and cut into strips. Mix the capsicum, pine nuts, capers, balsamic vinegar and oil.
3 Spread the cream cheese over the toasts and top with capsicum and caper mix. Makes 8

Tomato (back), Sardine (middle) and Capsicum (front) Bruschetta

NUTRIENTS per serve

Energy	2650kJ
Energy	633cal
Total fat	27.0g
Saturated fat	7.6g
Monounsaturated fat	12.0g
Polyunsaturated fat	5.6g
Protein	28.0g
Carbohydrate	69.0g
Fibre	7.6g
Sodium	321mg
Cholesterol	36mg

STAR INGREDIENT

SUNFLOWER OIL contains fat that is predominantly polyunsaturated. It is one of the richest oilseed sources of vitamin E. Sunflower oil has a mild flavour and can be used both for cooking and in salads.

NUTRIENTS per serve

Energy	2039kJ
Energy	487cal
Total fat	21.7g
Saturated fat	6.0g
Monounsaturated fat	6.5g
Polyunsaturated fat	5.1g
Protein	31.7g
Carbohydrate	40.7g
Fibre	3.8g
Sodium	621mg
Cholesterol	65.75mg

Vegetable Lasagna Stacks with Pesto

PREP TIME 40 minutes   COOKING TIME 5 minutes

Pesto
2 cloves garlic
2 tablespoons pine nuts, toasted
I cup fresh basil leaves
2 tablespoons finely grated parmesan
2 tablespoons extra virgin olive oil

375g fresh lasagna sheets
50g baby spinach leaves
4 large vine ripened tomatoes, cut into thick slices
6 large bocconcini, cut into thick slices
8 fresh basil leaves

I To make the pesto Put the garlic, pine nuts, basil leaves and parmesan in a food processor and process until coarsely chopped.
2 With the motor running, gradually add the oil and process until the mixture becomes a smooth paste.
3 Cut the lasagna sheets into twelve 8cm squares. Cook in a large pot of rapidly boiling water until al dente (cooked, but still with a bite to them). Drain well.
4 Put one sheet in the centre of each plate, top each with a couple of spinach leaves, a slice each of tomato and bocconcini, a fresh basil leaf and a spoonful of pesto.
5 Top with another sheet of lasagna and layer as before, finishing with a layer of lasagna. Each stack should have two complete layers.
6 Place a generous spoonful of pesto on top of each stack and serve immediately.
Serves 4

Moroccan Lamb Pizza

PREP TIME 30 minutes   COOKING TIME 20 minutes

I tablespoon sunflower oil
I red onion, finely chopped
2 cloves garlic, crushed
225g lean lamb mince
1/2 cup canned crushed tomatoes
I teaspoon ground cumin
I teaspoon ground coriander
1/2 teaspoon cinnamon
I tablespoon chopped fresh coriander
I tablespoon lemon juice
4 single serve, 97% fat free pizza bases

2 tablespoons pine nuts, toasted
120g reduced fat mozzarella, grated
I cup fresh mint leaves
I cup fresh flat leaf parsley
cracked black pepper
2 tablespoons mango chutney

Raita (yoghurt relish)
I cup reduced fat natural yoghurt
I Lebanese cucumber, grated
I tablespoon fresh mint, chopped

I Heat the oil in a fry pan, add the onion and I clove of crushed garlic and cook over a medium heat for I minute. Add the lamb and cook until the lamb is browned, breaking the meat up with a fork. Drain any excess oil from the pan. Add the tomatoes, cumin, ground coriander and cinnamon and cook for 5 minutes. Stir in the fresh coriander and 2 teaspoons lemon juice.
2 Preheat oven to 200°C. Spread the lamb topping over the pizza bases and sprinkle with pine nuts and mozzarella. Bake for 10 minutes or until the cheese has melted and the pizzas are heated through.
3 To make the raita Mix the yoghurt, grated cucumber, remaining crushed clove of garlic and chopped mint in a bowl.
4 Toss the mint and parsley leaves in the remaining lemon juice and season with pepper. Serve the pizzas topped with the herb leaves, raita and chutney. Serves 4

NUTRIENTS per serve

Energy	1558kJ
Energy	372cal
Total fat	24.0g
Saturated fat	8.7g
Monounsaturated fat	8.1g
Polyunsaturated fat	5.5g
Protein	31.0g
Carbohydrate	8.4g
Fibre	5.6g
Sodium	237mg
Cholesterol	50mg

TIP

WONTON WRAPPERS are thin pieces of pliable, pasta-like dough. They can be used to wrap well-flavoured sweet or savoury fillings. Keep wrappers covered to prevent them from drying out and, once opened, store in the fridge for 3-4 days only. Wonton wrappers are available fresh or frozen from Asian food stores, or frozen from some supermarkets.

NUTRIENTS per serve

Energy	1541kJ
Energy	367cal
Total fat	6.3g
Saturated fat	1.1g
Monounsaturated fat	2.3g
Polyunsaturated fat	2.0g
Protein	37.0g
Carbohydrate	28.0g
Fibre	3.0g
Sodium	342mg
Cholesterol	224mg

Chicken Satay with Crunchy Cabbage Salad

PREP TIME **40 minutes + soaking** COOKING TIME **20 minutes**

400g skinless chicken breast fillet
2 teaspoons peanut oil

1 1/2 tablespoons sweet chilli sauce
1 1/2 tablespoons lemon juice

Satay sauce
2 tablespoons peanut oil
2 cloves garlic, crushed
1 onion, finely chopped
1/4 cup peanut butter
270ml reduced fat coconut milk

Crunchy cabbage salad
1/4 Chinese cabbage, finely shredded
1 carrot, finely shredded
1 red capsicum, cut into fine strips
2 tablespoons sesame seeds, toasted

1 Soak 12 bamboo skewers in cold water for 20 minutes.
2 Cut the chicken into thin strips then thread onto skewers.
3 Lightly brush the skewers with oil and put on a foil-lined grill tray. Grill under a high heat, turning a couple of times during cooking until the chicken is tender.
4 To make the satay sauce Heat the oil in a small pot, add the garlic and onion and cook over a medium heat for 5 minutes or until golden. Add the peanut butter, coconut milk, sweet chilli sauce and lemon juice and simmer for 10 minutes or until the sauce thickens.
5 To make the cabbage salad Put the cabbage, carrot, capsicum and sesame seeds in a bowl and toss to combine.
6 To serve, place mounds of salad onto plates, top with chicken skewers and drizzle with the satay sauce. Serves 4

Prawn and Ginger Ravioli

PREP TIME **30 minutes** COOKING TIME **15 minutes**

600g green prawns, peeled and deveined
1 clove garlic, chopped
1 tablespoon grated fresh ginger
2 spring onions, finely sliced
200g wonton wrappers
fresh coriander sprigs, to garnish

Dressing
1 small red chilli, finely sliced
1 tablespoon fish sauce
2 teaspoons grated palm sugar
2 teaspoons lime juice
1 tablespoon peanut oil

1 Finely chop the prawns. Place the prawns, garlic, ginger and spring onions in a bowl and mix to combine.
2 Put a heaped teaspoon of the mixture in the centre of a wonton wrapper, lightly brush the edges with water and top with another wrapper. Press the edges firmly together to seal. Repeat with the remaining filling and wrappers.
3 Cook the ravioli in batches in a large pot of rapidly boiling water for 5 minutes. Drain well and transfer to serving plates.
4 To make the dressing Put the chilli, fish sauce, palm sugar, lime juice and peanut oil in a jug and whisk to combine.
5 Drizzle the dressing over the ravioli and serve topped with sprigs of fresh coriander. Serves 4

Main Meal Salads

Who says a salad can't satisfy? Not us. For those days when you just can't face slaving over a hot pot, we say make a salad and take in some sunshine. Our main meal salads will help you make healthy choices for hot days, and be happy you did so.

Thai Beef Salad

PREP TIME **30 minutes** COOKING TIME **10 minutes**

500g rump steak
black pepper
1 small red chilli, finely chopped
2 tablespoons lime juice
2 tablespoons fish sauce
2 tablespoons grated palm sugar or brown sugar
1 teaspoon sesame oil
1/4 Chinese cabbage, finely shredded
1 cup fresh coriander sprigs
1 cup fresh mint sprigs
100g snow peas, trimmed
1 Lebanese cucumber, sliced
1 small red onion, thinly sliced
200g cherry tomatoes, halved

1 Trim any excess fat and sinew from the steak. Season with black pepper.
2 Cook the steak on a lightly oiled chargrill for a few minutes until medium rare. Remove and rest for 10 minutes before slicing across the grain into thin strips.
3 Put the chilli, lime juice, fish sauce, palm sugar and sesame oil in a jug and whisk to combine.
4 Combine the cabbage, half the coriander, the mint, snow peas, cucumber, onion and tomatoes on a large salad platter or individual plates.
5 Top with the sliced steak, drizzle with dressing and garnish with the remaining coriander. Serves 4

Chargrilled Calamari and Bean Mash Salad

PREP TIME **20 minutes + marinating** COOKING TIME **10 minutes**

4 large calamari tubes, cleaned
100ml extra virgin olive oil
6 cloves garlic, crushed
3 small red chillies, finely sliced
2 tablespoons fresh oregano, chopped
1 sprig rosemary
2 x 300g cans cannellini beans, rinsed and drained
4 spring onions, finely sliced
2 tablespoons fresh flat leaf parsley
2 tablespoons lemon juice
rocket leaves, to serve

1 Slit each calamari tube along one side with a sharp knife, cut into large pieces and using a sharp knife score the underside in a diamond pattern but do not cut all the way through. Put 25ml of olive oil, 3 cloves garlic, 2 red chillies and the oregano in a bowl with the calamari pieces, cover and marinate in the refrigerator for 1-3 hours.
2 Put 75ml of the oil, rosemary, 3 cloves garlic and 1 chilli in a small pot and heat gently until the garlic just starts to turn golden. Strain the flavoured oil and set aside.
3 Put the beans in another pot and heat through. Transfer half the beans to a food processor. In a slow steady stream, pour the flavoured oil into the beans with the motor running. Fold the remaining whole beans into the pureed mixture. Set aside to keep warm. Discard the ingredients used to flavour the oil.
4 Heat a chargrill until very hot, drain the excess oil from the calamari and chargrill it over a very high heat for a couple of minutes or until just cooked.
5 Fold the spring onions and parsley through the bean mixture, put a generous mound on each plate and top with calamari pieces. Drizzle with lemon juice and serve with rocket. Serves 4-6

Thai Fish and Mango Salad

PREP TIME **25 minutes**	COOKING TIME **10 minutes**

2 small mangoes
2 Lebanese cucumbers
1 red capsicum, roasted, peeled and
    cut into thin strips
2 tablespoons fresh mint sprigs
2 tablespoons fresh coriander sprigs
80ml lime juice
1 teaspoon fresh ginger, grated
2 tablespoons fish sauce

2 tablespoons sweet chilli sauce
1 tablespoon grated light palm sugar
    or brown sugar
4 fillets (about 260g) blue eye cod
1 tablespoon peanut oil
2 tablespoons unsalted peanuts,
    roughly chopped

1 Peel the mangoes and slice the flesh into thin strips. Run a vegetable peeler down the length of the cucumber to form long ribbons and put in a bowl with the capsicum, mint and coriander. Toss, cover and refrigerate while preparing the rest of the salad.
2 Put the lime juice, ginger, fish sauce, sweet chilli sauce and palm sugar in a jug and whisk to combine.
3 Preheat a chargrill, lightly brush the fish fillets with the peanut oil and cook over a high heat for 3-4 minutes on each side or until cooked. Place some of the salad on each plate and top with fish fillets.
4 Drizzle the dressing over the fish and salad. Serve sprinkled with peanuts.
Serves 4

NUTRIENTS per serve

Energy	1097kJ
Energy	262cal
Total fat	12.0g
Saturated fat	2.3g
Monounsaturated fat	5.0g
Polyunsaturated fat	3.6g
Protein	18.0g
Carbohydrate	20.0g
Fibre	3.5g
Sodium	768mg
Cholesterol	46mg

TIP

To benefit from maximum flavour and nutritional value, fish should be bought and eaten as fresh as possible. Look for whole fish with bright, bulging eyes and flesh that is firm and resilient to touch. Fish fillets should be white or tinged with natural pinkness. Fish that has traces of discolouration or an unpleasant aroma should not be purchased: all fish should have a pleasant, fresh smell.

STAR INGREDIENT

MANGOES are an excellent source of carotene, which is converted to vitamin A in the body, and vitamin C. They contribute small quantities of other vitamins, as well as minerals such as potassium. Mangoes are a summer fruit but canned mango can be used in recipes as a substitute in other seasons.

NUTRIENTS per serve

Energy	2403kJ
Energy	574cal
Total fat	13.0g
Saturated fat	3.2g
Monounsaturated fat	5.7g
Polyunsaturated fat	2.1g
Protein	39.0g
Carbohydrate	76.0g
Fibre	10.0g
Sodium	793mg
Cholesterol	82mg

STAR INGREDIENT

CASHEW NUTS, like most seeds and other nuts, contain predominantly monounsaturated and polyunsaturated fats. They are a good source of protein, B group vitamins and vitamin E. Store cashews in a glass jar in the refrigerator to keep them fresh.

NUTRIENTS per serve

Energy	1724kJ
Energy	412cal
Total fat	18.0g
Saturated fat	2.5g
Monounsaturated fat	8.9g
Polyunsaturated fat	3.3g
Protein	17.0g
Carbohydrate	46.0g
Fibre	5.9g
Sodium	578mg
Cholesterol	0.67mg

Oregano Lamb and Couscous Salad

PREP TIME 20 minutes + marinating   COOKING TIME 15 minutes

500g lamb loin
2 cloves garlic, crushed
1 teaspoon ground cinnamon
1 teaspoon ground allspice
2 tablespoons lemon juice
1 teaspoon honey
1 tablespoon olive oil
2 tablespoons fresh oregano, chopped

1 cup couscous
500ml reduced salt chicken stock
400g can chickpeas, rinsed and drained
200g cherry tomatoes, halved
2 cups fresh flat leaf parsley, roughly chopped
1 cup raisins
2 oranges, cut into segments

1 Trim the lamb loin of all excess fat and sinew. Put the garlic, cinnamon, allspice, lemon juice, honey, olive oil and oregano in a jug and whisk to combine. Pour over the lamb, cover and marinate in the refrigerator for 4 hours or overnight.
2 Put the couscous in a bowl. Bring the chicken stock to the boil and pour over the couscous. Allow to stand for 10 minutes or until all the liquid is absorbed.
3 Lightly oil a chargrill or barbecue and cook the marinated lamb loin over a medium high heat for about 10 minutes or until medium rare. Allow to stand for 5 minutes before slicing.
4 Fold the lamb, chickpeas, tomatoes, parsley, raisins and oranges through the salad and serve. Serves 4

Hokkien Noodle, Mushroom and Cashew Salad

PREP TIME 30 minutes + standing   COOKING TIME 5 minutes

4 (15g) dried shiitake mushrooms
125ml boiling water
400g fresh hokkien noodles
100g enoki mushrooms
150g oyster mushrooms
200g button mushrooms, halved

4 spring onions, finely sliced
2 cloves garlic, crushed
2 tablespoons sweet chilli sauce
2 tablespoons reduced salt soy sauce
100g unsalted cashews, roasted
2 tablespoons sesame seeds

1 Put the shiitake mushrooms in a bowl, cover with boiling water and allow to stand for 25 minutes or until the mushrooms are soft. Drain and reserve the liquid. Remove the stalks from the mushrooms and discard. Cut the caps into thin slices.
2 Gently separate the hokkien noodles and put in a large bowl. Cover with boiling water and allow to stand for 2 minutes then drain well.
3 Separate the enoki mushrooms into small bunches and cut off any dry ends. Toss the shiitake, enoki, oyster and button mushrooms with the spring onions.
4 Put the garlic, sweet chilli sauce, soy sauce and reserved mushroom liquid in a small pot and simmer for a few minutes until reduced and slightly thickened. Pour over the mushrooms and toss to coat.
5 Toss the noodles, dressed mushrooms, cashews and sesame seeds together in a bowl and combine well. Transfer to serving bowls. Serves 4

NUTRIENTS per serve

Energy	1115kJ
Energy	266cal
Total fat	6.0g
Saturated fat	1.3g
Monounsaturated fat	3.0g
Polyunsaturated fat	0.7g
Protein	37.0g
Carbohydrate	15.3g
Fibre	3.1g
Sodium	644mg
Cholesterol	249mg

Summer Prawn and Avocado Salad

PREP TIME **30 minutes** COOKING TIME **20 minutes**

450g sweet potato, peeled and cut into small pieces
olive oil cooking spray
1 large iceberg lettuce, sliced
50g rocket leaves, washed
50g snow pea sprouts, washed
150g snow peas, trimmed
1kg cooked king prawns, peeled, deveined and tails left intact

1 large ripe avocado, chopped
cracked black pepper to serve

Dressing
2 tablespoons lime juice
2 tablespoons fresh dill, chopped
2 tablespoons reduced salt tomato sauce
2 tablespoons rice wine vinegar
2 tablespoons reduced fat natural yoghurt

1 Preheat oven to 200°C. Put the sweet potato in a large baking dish, spray lightly with olive oil spray and cook for 20 minutes or until soft.
2 Put the lettuce rounds onto individual plates. Top with rocket and snow pea sprouts.
3 Steam the snow peas until tender, rinse under cold water and drain well.
4 Arrange snow peas and sweet potato on top of the greens, then top with prawns and chopped avocado.
5 To make the dressing Put the lime juice, dill, tomato sauce, rice wine vinegar and yoghurt in a bowl and whisk to combine. The dressing should be of pouring consistency. If it is too thick add 1-2 tablespoons cold water.
6 Drizzle the dressing over the salad and garnish with a few extra snow pea sprouts and cracked black pepper. Serves 4-6

This salad looks great served on a large platter if you are entertaining.

STAR INGREDIENT
AVOCADOS contain high levels of monounsaturated fats and are an excellent source of vitamins C and E, and folate. Try avocado as a sandwich spread instead of butter or margarine.

NUTRIENTS per serve

Energy	875kJ
Energy	209cal
Total fat	3.1g
Saturated fat	0.7g
Monounsaturated fat	1.1g
Polyunsaturated fat	0.5g
Protein	26.0g
Carbohydrate	19.0g
Fibre	3.0g
Sodium	632mg
Cholesterol	50mg

TIP

Try to get into the habit of eating at least two fish (preferably oily fish) meals each week. Good examples are salmon, mullet, gemfish, trout and mackerel. These fish are all high in beneficial marine omega-3 fatty acids.

NUTRIENTS per serve

Energy	633kJ
Energy	151cal
Total fat	1.3g
Saturated fat	0.3g
Monounsaturated fat	0.3g
Polyunsaturated fat	0.3g
Protein	20.0g
Carbohydrate	28.0g
Fibre	5.0g
Sodium	230mg
Cholesterol	70mg

Asian Chicken and Kaffir Lime Salad

PREP TIME **20 minutes** COOKING TIME **15 minutes**

2-3 (about 400g) skinless chicken breast fillets
4 kaffir lime leaves, finely shredded
1 lime, sliced
100g Chinese (mung bean) vermicelli
250g green beans, halved
1 cup fresh coriander leaves
1 cup fresh Thai basil leaves, shredded

4 spring onions, thinly sliced
2 tablespoons fried shallots

Dressing
2 tablespoons fish sauce
2 tablespoons lime juice
2 tablespoons palm sugar, grated

1 Put chicken breast fillets in a large deep fry pan, add the kaffir lime leaves and lime slices and cover with water. Bring to the boil, reduce the heat to a very slow simmer and poach the chicken for 15 minutes or until tender. Drain the chicken, reserving 60ml of the liquid. Allow chicken to cool slightly then shred finely using your fingers.
2 While the chicken is cooking put the vermicelli in a bowl and cover with boiling water. Allow to stand for 5-10 minutes or until tender then drain well. Cook the beans until tender then drain.
3 Put the chicken, vermicelli, coriander, basil leaves, green beans, spring onions and shallots into a bowl and toss to combine.
4 To make the dressing Put the reserved cooking liquid, fish sauce, lime juice and palm sugar in a jug and whisk well. Pour over the salad and toss to combine.
Serves 4

Warm Potato and Salmon Salad

PREP TIME **30 minutes** COOKING TIME **45 minutes**

600g salmon fillet
500g baby (new) potatoes, halved
olive oil cooking spray
100g baby corn
100g baby spinach leaves, washed and halved lengthwise

100g semi-dried tomatoes

Dressing
4 tablespoons reduced fat natural yoghurt
3 tablespoons sweet chilli sauce
2 tablespoons lemon juice

1 Preheat oven to 200°C.
2 Remove the skin from the salmon fillet and then use tweezers to remove any bones. Cut the salmon into large cubes.
3 Put the potatoes in a large baking dish, lightly spray with olive oil spray and cook for 30 minutes, turning a couple of times during cooking.
4 Add the baby corn to the potatoes and cook for 10 minutes or until the potatoes and corn are tender. Turn the oven off and keep the vegetables warm. Lightly spray a chargrill with olive oil spray and cook the salmon cubes over a high heat for 3-4 minutes or until just tender and golden.
5 To make the dressing Put the yoghurt, sweet chilli sauce and lemon juice in a small jug and whisk well.
6 Put the potatoes, corn, spinach and semi-dried tomatoes in a bowl and toss to combine. Arrange the salad on individual plates, top with hot salmon pieces and drizzle with the dressing. Serves 4

NUTRIENTS per serve

Energy	2321kJ
Energy	555cal
Total fat	34.0g
Saturated fat	8.4g
Monounsaturated fat	16.0g
Polyunsaturated fat	6.9g
Protein	18.0g
Carbohydrate	45.0g
Fibre	12.0g
Sodium	644mg
Cholesterol	32mg

TIP

Foods high in fibre include legumes, fruit, vegetables, wholegrain breads and cereals. Aim for around 30g of fibre a day to help keep you regular.

NUTRIENTS per serve

Energy	969kJ
Energy	231cal
Total fat	8.8g
Saturated fat	0.9g
Monounsaturated fat	1.2g
Polyunsaturated fat	4.0g
Protein	17.0g
Carbohydrate	20.0g
Fibre	7.6g
Sodium	31mg
Cholesterol	0.83mg

Ricotta and Beetroot Salad with Pita Crisps

PREP TIME **20 minutes** COOKING TIME **30 minutes**

300g wedge reduced fat ricotta cheese
1/2 teaspoon cayenne pepper
olive oil cooking spray
2 wholemeal pita pockets, split in half and cut into triangles
2 medium beetroot, boiled until tender
2 pears
1 avocado

1 bunch rocket
4 tablespoons walnuts, roasted

Dressing
1 1/2 tablespoons raspberry vinegar
cracked black pepper
2 tablespoons extra virgin olive oil

1 Preheat oven to 250°C. Put the ricotta on a baking tray lined with non stick baking paper, sprinkle with cayenne and spray lightly with olive oil spray. Bake for 20 minutes or until golden brown. Allow to cool slightly before breaking into large pieces.
2 Put the pita triangles on another tray, put under a medium grill and cook until crisp.
3 Peel the beetroot and cut into small pieces. Use gloves to stop your hands from turning pink. Thinly slice the pears. Peel and chop the avocado.
4 Arrange the rocket, beetroot, pears and avocado on individual plates. Top with ricotta.
5 To make the dressing Whisk together the vinegar, pepper and oil and drizzle over each salad. Sprinkle with coarsely chopped walnuts.
6 Serve with stacks of pita crisps on the side. Serves **4**

Spiced Pumpkin, Lentil and Tofu Salad

PREP TIME **15 minutes** COOKING TIME **45 minutes**

300g pumpkin, cut into 2cm cubes
300g cauliflower, cut into florets
1 cup brown lentils, rinsed
1 tablespoon soybean oil
3 large onions, sliced
1 red capsicum, thinly sliced
300g firm tofu, cut into small cubes
1/2 teaspoon cinnamon

1/2 teaspoon allspice
pinch saffron
1/4 cup sunflower seeds
1/2 cup fresh mint, chopped
100g reduced fat natural yoghurt
harissa (North African chilli paste), to serve

1 Steam or microwave the pumpkin and cauliflower until tender and drain well. Put the lentils in a large pot of water and simmer for 20 minutes or until tender; drain.
2 Heat the oil in a large fry pan, add the onions and capsicum and cook over a medium heat for 20 minutes or until caramelised. Remove half the onions from the pan and set aside.
3 Add the tofu, cinnamon, allspice, saffron and sunflower seeds to the pan with 1 tablespoon of water and cook over a medium heat until all the water is absorbed and the tofu is golden.
4 Put the lentils, tofu mixture, pumpkin, cauliflower and mint in a bowl and gently mix to combine.
5 Serve the salad on individual plates topped with fried onions, a dollop of yoghurt and a small spoonful of harissa. Serves **4-6**

The heart healthy shopping list

Looking after your heart doesn't mean searching for special ingredients. Here's what to stock up on, and some good reasons why.

Grains and cereals
◆ choose mainly wholegrain or wholemeal varieties
◆ pasta (dried wholemeal and plain spaghetti, fettuccine, penne, macaroni, lasagna sheets)
◆ noodles (cellophane, rice, hokkien, udon, egg, soba)
◆ rice (white, brown, long or short grain, arborio, jasmine, basmati, wild)
◆ grains (couscous, cornmeal, sago, tapioca, buckwheat, bulgar, pearl barley, rye, rolled oats, bran)
◆ flours (plain high-fibre white, wholemeal, self-raising, rice, cornflour)
◆ high-fibre breakfast cereals

Vegetables and fruit
◆ fresh vegetables and fruit
◆ canned and bottled vegetables are convenient and may include artichoke hearts, asparagus, bamboo shoots, beetroot, carrots, corn kernels, gherkins, mushrooms, olives, peas, tomatoes and water chestnuts but avoid vegetables preserved in brine or butter sauce
◆ dried fruit and fruit packed in natural juice is handy to use for desserts, smoothies, snacks and as a breakfast cereal topping

Canned and dried legumes
◆ dried, canned and vacuum-sealed chickpeas, lentils, split peas, black beans, kidney beans, soybeans, cannellini beans, Mexican chilli beans, four-bean mix and baked beans

Nuts and seeds
◆ all nuts and seeds but choose unsalted nuts and store them in an airtight container after opening

Fish and seafood
◆ fresh fish or shellfish - cook straight away or store in the freezer in sealed plastic bags and use within 3 months
◆ all canned fish are good sources of marine omega-3 polyunsaturated fats (ie salmon, sardines, herring, kipper, tuna fillets) but fish in brine is higher in sodium (salt) than fish in spring water or oil
◆ fish canned in canola oil is high in plant omega-3 fatty acids which appear to help reduce the risk of heart disease

Meat and poultry
◆ red meat is particularly rich in iron, zinc and vitamin B12
◆ white meat and poultry also contain these nutrients but in smaller amounts
◆ choose lean or trimmed varieties of red meat, white meat and poultry
◆ where possible, select cuts of meat displaying the Heart Foundation "Tick" of approval

Dairy
◆ choose low or reduced fat dairy products such as low or reduced fat milk, low or reduced fat plain yoghurt, low or reduced fat fruit yoghurt, low or reduced fat custard, a reduced fat hard cheese or sliced cheese, cottage cheese, reduced fat ricotta, reduced fat feta and light or reduced fat cream cheese
◆ low or reduced fat ice-cream, frozen yoghurt and soy-based frozen desserts containing less than 5% fat

Eggs
◆ our recipes are based on 48g-50g eggs
◆ eggs high in plant omega-3 polyunsaturated fats are available

Margarine spreads
◆ use margarine spreads instead of butter or dairy blends
◆ plant sterol enriched margarine spread is good for people with high blood cholesterol

Liquid stock
◆ reduced salt stocks such as reduced salt stock cubes, stock powders or liquid stock in the handy long-life packs, (eg reduced salt vegetable, beef, chicken or fish stock)

Reduced fat evaporated milk and light coconut milk

◆ use as a substitute for cream and regular coconut milk to substantially reduce the saturated fat content of a recipe

Oils

◆ polyunsaturated and monounsaturated oils can help lower blood cholesterol levels, although polyunsaturated fats tend to have a greater effect than monounsaturated fats
◆ choose polyunsaturated oils (eg safflower, sunflower, corn, soybean and grapeseed oils) and monounsaturated oils (eg including canola, olive, macadamia, peanut and mustard seed oils)
◆ canola and soybean oils are high in alpha-linolenic acid

Dressings

◆ use salad dressings and mayonnaise made from oils such as canola, sunflower, soybean and olive oils

Sauces and condiments

◆ tomato sauces (paste*, puree*, pasta sauce*, ketchup*)
◆ salt reduced soy sauce*, black bean*, hoisin*, oyster*, fish*, Worcestershire*, barbecue*, sweet chilli, Tabasco, plum, apricot
◆ citrus juice (lemon, lime, orange)
◆ vinegar (white, brown, rice, balsamic)
◆ cooking wine (red, white, mirin, sherry)
◆ condiments like seeded mustard, English mustard, horseradish, wasabi, mint jelly, chutney and relish
◆ remember to refrigerate sauces and condiments after opening

*These sauces are high in salt so where possible, choose the reduced salt variety and use in small quantities only (especially if you suffer from high blood pressure)

Herbs and spices

◆ these add flavour to meals without the addition of salt: basil, cayenne pepper, chilli, cinnamon, coriander, cumin, curry, garlic, ginger, lemon grass, mint, nutmeg, oregano, paprika, parsley, rosemary, saffron, thyme and turmeric
◆ the list is endless: choose and use as desired!

 **Heart Foundation**

For further information on any heart health issue, ring the Heart Foundation's **HEARTLINE** on 1300 36 27 87 (for the cost of a local call).

Dinner

Each of our dinners is packed with nutritious fresh ingredients that won't take precious hours to prepare. There are so many delicious dishes to choose from! So whether you're cooking a meal for the family - or entertaining good friends - you'll enjoy making and sharing these beautiful recipes.

Steamed Fish Rolls with Tomato Vinaigrette

PREP TIME **20 minutes** + chilling   COOKING TIME **10 minutes**

4 (about 700g) boneless, skinless white fish fillets
2 tablespoons grape seed oil
2 cloves garlic, crushed
6 spring onions, chopped
1 cup fresh wholemeal breadcrumbs
1/2 cup fresh basil leaves, chopped

1 cup fresh flat leaf parsley, chopped
1 teaspoon lemon zest
2 tablespoons lemon juice
250ml tomato juice
2 tablespoons white wine vinegar
1 tablespoon brown sugar

1 Cut the fish fillets in half lengthwise, following the natural centre line.
2 Heat 1 tablespoon of the oil in a large non stick fry pan, add the garlic and spring onions and cook over a medium heat for 3 minutes or until the spring onions are soft. Put in a food processor with the breadcrumbs, half the basil, half the parsley and the lemon zest and juice. Process to combine.
3 Divide the stuffing into eight equal portions and roll into oblong shapes, put a piece on the end of each piece of fish and roll up to enclose the filling. Secure with a toothpick or piece of string. Cover and refrigerate for 30 minutes.
4 Finely chop the remaining basil and parsley and put into a saucepan with the tomato juice, vinegar and brown sugar. Cook over a low heat until warm.
5 Put the fish rolls in a large bamboo steamer lined with baking paper. Cover and put over a wok of simmering water, making sure the base of the steamer does not touch the water. Steam for 10 minutes or until the fish is tender and the stuffing heated through.
6 Serve the fish rolls drizzled with tomato vinaigrette and a crisp green salad. Serves 4

Paella

PREP TIME **30 minutes**   COOKING TIME **40 minutes**

3 tablespoons olive oil
2-3 (about 300g) skinless chicken thigh fillets, cut into thick strips
1 onion, chopped
1 1/3 cups short-grain rice
3 vine ripened tomatoes, chopped
pinch saffron
400g can chickpeas, rinsed and drained
150g green beans
1 red capsicum, sliced

750ml reduced salt chicken stock
12 black mussels, hairy beards removed
500g green prawns, peeled, deveined and tails left intact
1 calamari tube (about 360g), cut into rings
2 tablespoons fresh flat leaf parsley, chopped
lemon wedges, to serve

1 Heat the oil in a large, deep fry pan or paella pan, add the chicken and cook over a medium heat just until browned. Remove and drain on absorbent paper.
2 Add the onion to the pan and cook over a medium heat until soft and golden. Add the rice, tomato and saffron and cook until the rice is translucent and cooked.
3 Return the chicken to the pan with the chickpeas, green beans, capsicum and stock; cook uncovered for 15 minutes.
4 Stir the seafood into the rice and continue cooking without stirring for 10 minutes or until the seafood is just tender and the base of the rice is crisp.
5 Sprinkle with parsley and serve with lemon wedges. Serves 4-6

NUTRIENTS per serve

Energy	1519kJ
Energy	363cal
Total fat	15.0g
Saturated fat	3.1g
Monounsaturated fat	4.1g
Polyunsaturated fat	7.0g
Protein	40.0g
Carbohydrate	16.0g
Fibre	3.0g
Sodium	401mg
Cholesterol	122mg

STAR INGREDIENT

SKINLESS LEAN CHICKEN is a suitable food for a healthy eating pattern. Chicken and turkey are both excellent sources of protein, niacin and phosphorus.

NUTRIENTS per serve

Energy	2206kJ
Energy	527cal
Total fat	14.0g
Saturated fat	2.2g
Monounsaturated fat	7.8g
Polyunsaturated fat	2.1g
Protein	48.0g
Carbohydrate	52.0g
Fibre	6.5g
Sodium	668mg
Cholesterol	269mg

Crisp Skin Salmon Fillets with Bean Puree and Mango Salsa

PREP TIME **20 minutes** COOKING TIME **10 minutes**

Mango salsa
1 large mango, diced
2 small Lebanese cucumbers, diced
1 tablespoon baby capers, rinsed
1 small red chilli, seeded and
   finely chopped
2 spring onions, sliced
1 tablespoon lemon juice
1 teaspoon olive oil
1 tablespoon fresh coriander, chopped

Beans and salmon
2 x 400g cannellini beans,
   rinsed and drained
200ml reduced salt chicken stock
1 bay leaf
2 cloves garlic, crushed
4 x 150g salmon fillets with skin
1 1/2 tablespoons peanut oil

1 To make the salsa Put all the ingredients in a bowl and mix gently to combine.
2 Put the cannellini beans, stock, bay leaf and garlic in a pot and bring to the boil. Reduce the heat and simmer for 5 minutes or until heated through. Remove the bay leaf and discard, transfer the mixture to a food processor or blender and process until smooth and creamy.
3 Pat the salmon fillets dry using absorbent paper. Heat the oil in a large non stick fry pan and cook the salmon fillets over a medium high heat for a few minutes, skin side down, until the skin is crisp and golden. Turn over and cook the other side for a couple of minutes or until just cooked through.
4 Serve the salmon fillets leaning up against a mound of bean puree and topped with mango salsa. Serves 4

STAR INGREDIENT
CANNELLINI BEANS contain good quality protein, fibre and B group vitamins as well as a range of minerals, including zinc. They are a delicious addition to salads, soups, stews and casseroles.

NUTRIENTS per serve

Energy	931kJ
Energy	222cal
Total fat	9.8g
Saturated fat	1.5g
Monounsaturated fat	4.0g
Polyunsaturated fat	2.5g
Protein	13.0g
Carbohydrate	24.0g
Fibre	14.0g
Sodium	621mg
Cholesterol	105mg

NUTRIENTS per serve

Energy	2500kJ
Energy	597cal
Total fat	14.0g
Saturated fat	10.0g
Monounsaturated fat	2.0g
Polyunsaturated fat	0.5g
Protein	42.0g
Carbohydrate	75.0g
Fibre	9.4g
Sodium	596mg
Cholesterol	62mg

TIP

Aim to include a large salad or serving of vegetables at every meal. Take a look at our Main Meal Salads or Vegetables and Side Dishes chapters for some great ideas.

TIP

Coconut milk is the liquid extracted from freshly grated and pressed coconut flesh. All coconut products, including the milk, are high in saturated fat so it is important to select a reduced fat or lite variety and use it sparingly.

NUTRIENTS per serve

Energy	1285kJ
Energy	307cal
Total fat	5.0g
Saturated fat	1.2g
Monounsaturated fat	1.6g
Polyunsaturated fat	1.6g
Protein	40.0g
Carbohydrate	24.0g
Fibre	7.8g
Sodium	307mg
Cholesterol	61mg

Light Chicken Curry with Jasmine Rice

PREP TIME 15 minutes COOKING TIME 30 minutes

400ml reduced fat coconut milk
250ml reduced salt chicken stock
2-3 tablespoons green curry paste
3 kaffir lime leaves, finely shredded
300g pumpkin, peeled and chopped
4 (about 500g) skinless chicken breast
   fillets, cut into small cubes
230g can bamboo shoots, drained
300g snake beans, chopped

300g broccoli, cut into florets
1 tablespoon fish sauce
1 tablespoon palm sugar, grated
2 tablespoons Thai basil leaves, torn

Jasmine rice
1 1/2 cup jasmine rice
2 stalks lemon grass, halved

1 Put the coconut milk, stock, green curry paste and kaffir lime leaves in wok or large pot and bring to the boil. Cook over a high heat until the sauce starts to thicken slightly. Add the pumpkin and simmer for 10 minutes or until it starts to soften
2 Add the chicken breast and bamboo shoots, reduce the heat and simmer for 10 minutes or until the chicken is tender. Add the snake beans, broccoli, fish sauce and palm sugar and cook uncovered until the vegetables are soft.
3 Remove from the heat and stir through half the basil leaves.
4 To make the jasmine rice Put the rice, lemon grass and 4 cups of water in a pot, bring to the boil and cook over a high heat until steam holes appear in the top of the rice. Reduce the heat to low, cover and cook over a low heat for 10 minutes or until all the liquid is absorbed and the rice is tender. Transfer rice to bowls, spoon over curry and scatter with remaining basil leaves. Serves 4

Rosemary Pork with Lentils and Apples

PREP TIME 20 minutes COOKING TIME 25 minutes

500g pork fillet
12 sprigs fresh rosemary
canola cooking spray
2 Granny Smith apples, peeled, cored
   and cut into 2cm thick wedges
2 tablespoons red wine vinegar

250ml reduced salt chicken or vegetable
   stock
1 tablespoon canola spread, melted
1/4 teaspoon ground cloves
1 cup red lentils
1 bay leaf

1 Preheat oven to 200°C. Trim any excess fat or sinew from the pork fillet. Cut the pork into 12 even slices and push a sprig of rosemary through the centre of each.
2 Lightly spray a non stick fry pan with canola spray, heat over a medium high heat until hot, then cook the pork in batches for a couple of minutes until browned all over. Transfer to a baking dish.
3 Put the apples in the fry pan and cook until browned. Transfer to the baking dish. Add the vinegar and stock to the pan, scraping the bottom to release any juices that may be stuck to the bottom. Pour over the pork and apple. Brush the apple with the melted canola and sprinkle with the ground cloves. Bake for 10 minutes or until the pork is tender, then rest it.
4 While the pork is cooking, put the lentils and bay leaf in a small pot, just cover with water and bring to the boil. Cook over a high heat for 15 minutes or until tender; drain and remove the bay leaf.
5 Serve the lentils topped with apples, pork and cooking juices. Serve with steamed green vegetables. Serves 4

Lamb Racks with Broad Bean and Pea Puree

PREP TIME **40 minutes** COOKING TIME **45 minutes**

NUTRIENTS per serve

Energy	1331kJ
Energy	318cal
Total fat	8.3g
Saturated fat	3.5g
Monounsaturated fat	2.9g
Polyunsaturated fat	0.6g
Protein	54.0g
Carbohydrate	5.5g
Fibre	11.0g
Sodium	317mg
Cholesterol	127mg

TIP

Not so long ago lamb was considered old fashioned and fatty but new breeding techniques are producing leaner varieties. The leanest cut of lamb is the backstrap or loin. Look for lean lamb cutlets displaying the Heart Foundation "Tick" of approval.

4 x 4 cutlet racks of lamb (about 750g)
2 cloves garlic, sliced
2 sprigs fresh rosemary, torn
$^1/_2$ cup mint jelly
2 tablespoons wholegrain mustard
2 tablespoons balsamic vinegar

Broad bean and pea puree
500g fresh or frozen broad beans, thawed and peeled
1 cup frozen mint peas
125ml reduced salt chicken stock

1 Preheat oven to 200°C. Trim any excess fat from the rack and any sinew away from the bones using a small sharp knife. Cut small slits in the lamb and put slices of garlic and torn sprigs of rosemary into each hole.
2 Put the mint jelly, mustard and balsamic vinegar into a small pot and bring to the boil. Brush the lamb racks with the glaze and put into a baking dish.
3 Roast the racks for 35-40 minutes for medium rare. Allow to stand for 5 minutes before cutting into cutlets.
4 To make the broad bean and pea puree While the lamb roasts, put the broad beans, peas and stock in a pot, bring to the boil then reduce the heat and simmer until the broad beans are soft and most of the liquid is absorbed. Mash until very smooth or put in a food processor and blend until smooth.
5 Serve the cutlets on a mound of broad bean puree, drizzle with the warmed glaze and serve with steamed or roasted baby potatoes. Serves 4

The puree will discolour on standing so do not make it too far in advance.

STAR INGREDIENT
BROAD BEANS may be eaten either fresh or dried. Fresh broad beans are a good source of dietary fibre and iron, as well as riboflavin and niacin (both B vitamins). Cooked broad beans have a luscious, creamy texture and loads of flavour.

Spicy Prawn and Scallop Spaghetti

PREP TIME **15 minutes**   COOKING TIME **20 minutes**

500g green prawns
250g scallops without roe
350g tubular spaghetti
30g olive oil spread
2 teaspoons olive oil
2 cloves garlic, crushed
3 spring onions, sliced
1 small red chilli, finely chopped

125ml dry white wine
2 large vine ripened tomatoes,
   seeded and finely chopped
1 teaspoon lemon zest
1 teaspoon orange zest
1 teaspoon white sugar
1 tablespoon chopped fresh chives

1 Peel and devein the prawns, leaving the tails intact. Pat the scallops dry with paper towel.
2 Cook the spaghetti in a large pot of rapidly boiling water until al dente (cooked but still with a bite to it). Drain, cover and keep warm.
3 Heat the olive oil spread and olive oil in a large, deep fry pan and cook the prawns and scallops in batches over a high heat just until tender. Remove and keep warm.
4 Add the garlic, onion and chilli to the pan and cook over a medium heat until the onion is soft. Stir in the wine and bring to the boil, stirring to release any juices that may be stuck to the bottom of the pan. Boil until reduced by half.
5 Add the tomatoes, zest, sugar and chives to the pan and cook just until the tomato is warmed through.
6 Add the prawns, scallops and spaghetti and toss to combine. Serve with crusty bread. Serves 4

Kangaroo on Mash with Cranberry Glaze

PREP TIME **20 minutes**   COOKING TIME **30 minutes**

500g kangaroo fillet
1 tablespoon finely cracked black pepper
canola cooking spray
250ml red wine
1/2 cup dried cranberries
3 tablespoons cranberry jelly
2 tablespoons balsamic vinegar
50g watercress

Mashed potato
500g potatoes for mashing
   (eg desiree or pontiac)
2 cloves garlic, crushed
60ml reduced fat evaporated milk
2 teaspoons extra virgin olive oil
brussels sprouts to serve

1 Preheat the oven to 200°C. Trim the kangaroo fillet of any excess fat or sinew. Roll the fillet in pepper, pressing firmly to coat evenly.
2 Spray a large non stick fry pan with canola spray and heat until hot. Add the kangaroo and brown all over. Transfer to a baking dish and roast for 20 minutes for medium rare. Remove, transfer to a tray and allow to stand for 10 minutes.
3 Add the red wine to the baking dish, stirring to release any juices that may be stuck to the bottom. Boil until reduced by half. Add the cranberries, cranberry jelly and balsamic vinegar and simmer for 10 minutes or until the sauce is thick enough to coat the back of a spoon.
4 To make the mashed potato   Cook the peeled potatoes in water until tender, drain and return to the pot with garlic, milk and oil. Cook over a low heat until hot then remove and coarsely mash.
5 Serve the sliced kangaroo fillet on top of the potato, topped with cranberry glaze and watercress. Serve brussels sprouts on the side. Serves 4

NUTRIENTS per serve

Energy	1944kJ
Energy	465cal
Total fat	3.5g
Saturated fat	0.6g
Monounsaturated fat	0.5g
Polyunsaturated fat	1.4g
Protein	43.0g
Carbohydrate	64.0g
Fibre	5.0g
Sodium	545mg
Cholesterol	207mg

TIP

Don't be afraid to try game meats: kangaroo, venison and hare are all rich in protein and low in saturated fat. Kangaroo is especially rich in iron and its strong flavour is well matched to fruit based sauces and glazes.

NUTRIENTS per serve

Energy	725kJ
Energy	173cal
Total fat	3.0g
Saturated fat	0.6g
Monounsaturated fat	1.8g
Polyunsaturated fat	0.3g
Protein	5.3g
Carbohydrate	20.0g
Fibre	3.2g
Sodium	66mg
Cholesterol	59mg

Vegetable and Chickpea Curry with Poppy Seed Rice

PREP TIME **30** minutes COOKING TIME **25** minutes

NUTRIENTS per serve

Energy	2017kJ
Energy	482cal
Total fat	12.0g
Saturated fat	1.7g
Monounsaturated fat	2.5g
Polyunsaturated fat	6.7g
Protein	12.0g
Carbohydrate	80.0g
Fibre	9.9g
Sodium	314mg
Cholesterol	0mg

2 tablespoons soybean oil
1 brown onion, thinly sliced
1 tablespoon grated fresh ginger
3 cloves garlic, crushed
3 long green chillies, finely chopped
1/2 teaspoon dried turmeric
2 teaspoons ground coriander
2 teaspoons garam masala
2 potatoes, cut into large cubes
2 carrots, cut into thick slices
2 zucchini, cut into thick slices

425g can chopped tomatoes
250ml reduced salt vegetable stock
400g can chickpeas, rinsed and drained
200g baby spinach leaves, washed
1 cup fresh or frozen peas

Poppy seed rice
1 1/2 cups basmati rice
2 tablespoons poppy seeds
microwave poppadoms to serve

1 Heat the oil in a large pot, add the onion and ginger and cook over a medium heat for 5 minutes or until soft. Add the garlic, chillies and spices and cook for 2 minutes or until fragrant.

2 Add the potatoes and carrots and cook until the vegetables are coated in the spices. Stir in the zucchini, tomatoes and stock and simmer. Reduce the heat and cook uncovered for 15 minutes or until the vegetables are tender and the curry has thickened slightly. Add the chickpeas and stir.

3 Add the chickpeas, spinach and peas; cook just until the spinach wilts and the chickpeas are soft.

4 To make the poppy seed rice Put the rice and poppy seeds in a pot, add 450ml of water and bring to the boil. Cook over a high heat until tunnels appear in the rice. Reduce the heat to very low, cover and allow to steam for 10 minutes or until the rice is tender and all the liquid is absorbed.

5 Serve the curry on top of the rice and accompany with microwaved poppadoms.
Serves 4

STAR INGREDIENT
CHICKPEAS have a nutty flavour and a pleasantly coarse texture. Dried chickpeas need soaking before cooking, but pre-cooked ones are widely available either canned or in vacuum packs. They are a great source of dietary fibre, and provide B group vitamins and phytoestrogens.

Slow Simmered Lamb Shanks with Couscous

NUTRIENTS per serve

Energy	1794kJ
Energy	430cal
Total fat	5.3g
Saturated fat	2.3g
Monounsaturated fat	1.6g
Polyunsaturated fat	0.5g
Protein	37.0g
Carbohydrate	47.0g
Fibre	6.4g
Sodium	165mg
Cholesterol	95mg

PREP TIME 20 minutes   COOKING TIME 1 hour 40 minutes

4 Frenched lamb shanks
   (ask your butcher to do this)
400g can chopped tomatoes
250ml red wine
1 bay leaf
6 sprigs fresh thyme
1 cinnamon stick

250g pumpkin, cut into large pieces
2 zucchini, cut into large pieces
8 dried apricots
8 dried prunes
1 cup couscous
2 tablespoons flaked almonds, toasted

1 Preheat the oven to 160°C. Heat a large fry pan over a high heat and sear the lamb shanks in batches until browned all over. Transfer to an ovenproof casserole dish.
2 Add the tomatoes, red wine, bay leaf, thyme and cinnamon stick. Cover and bake for 1 hour. Add the pumpkin, zucchini, apricots and prunes, uncover and cook for 30 minutes longer or until the vegetables are soft and the lamb begins to come away from the bone.
3 Put the couscous in a large bowl, pour over 500ml boiling water and allow to stand for 10 minutes or until all the liquid is absorbed.
4 Serve the lambs shanks in deep bowls on top of the couscous and garnished with flaked almonds. Serves 4

Smoked Salmon, Asparagus and Lemon Fettuccine

NUTRIENTS per serve

Energy	2104kJ
Energy	503cal
Total fat	16.0g
Saturated fat	1.9g
Monounsaturated fat	7.7g
Polyunsaturated fat	5.2g
Protein	24.0g
Carbohydrate	64.0g
Fibre	6.8g
Sodium	870mg
Cholesterol	24mg

PREP TIME 15 minutes   COOKING TIME 20 minutes

500g fettuccine
2 tablespoons extra virgin olive oil
pinch saffron
2 cloves garlic, crushed
1 teaspoon lemon zest
80ml lemon juice
1 tablespoon sugar
250ml reduced salt chicken stock
300g asparagus

4 spring onions, sliced
100g semi-dried tomatoes
300g smoked salmon or smoked ocean
   trout, torn into large pieces
200g baby spinach leaves, washed
50g pine nuts, toasted
1/4 cup chopped fresh dill
cracked black pepper to taste

1 Cook the fettuccine in a large pot of rapidly boiling water until al dente (cooked, but still with a bite to it) then drain well.
2 Put the olive oil, saffron, garlic, zest, juice, sugar and stock in a jug and whisk. Gently heat the mixture in a large, deep non stick fry pan until warm.
3 Cut the asparagus into 4cm pieces and simmer in the olive oil mixture until bright green and just tender. Add the spring onions, tomatoes and fettuccine and toss gently to heat through. Remove from the heat and gently toss through the smoked salmon or trout, spinach, pine nuts and dill. Season with cracked black pepper and serve immediately. Serves 6

Veal with Lemon, Crisp Sage and Cornmeal

PREP TIME 15 minutes COOKING TIME 15 minutes

NUTRIENTS per serve

Energy	1197kJ
Energy	286cal
Total fat	9.1g
Saturated fat	1.4g
Monounsaturated fat	5.7g
Polyunsaturated fat	1.2g
Protein	18.0g
Carbohydrate	29.0g
Fibre	3.5g
Sodium	683mg
Cholesterol	44mg

500ml reduced salt chicken stock
1 cup instant cornmeal
4 large veal escalopes
   (thin, boneless slices)
plain flour, for dusting
2 teaspoons olive oil
20g olive oil spread
80ml dry white wine
zest of 1 lemon
3 tablespoons lemon juice

1 cup frozen broad beans,
   thawed and peeled
1 tablespoon baby capers
12 fresh sage leaves
olive oil cooking spray
1 tablespoon balsamic vinegar
3 Roma tomatoes, cut into thick slices
cracked black pepper to taste

1 Bring the chicken stock to the boil in a medium pot. Gradually whisk in the cornmeal and cook over a medium heat for 8 minutes or until the cornmeal starts to come away from the side of the pot. Cover and keep warm.

2 Dust the veal escalopes in flour, shaking off any excess. Heat the olive oil and olive oil spread in a large, deep fry pan, add the veal and cook over a medium heat until golden brown on both sides. This will only take a couple of minutes on each side. Remove and keep warm.

3 Add the wine to the pan and bring to the boil, stirring to remove any juices that may be stuck to the bottom. Boil until reduced by half. Add the lemon zest, juice and broad beans and boil until the sauce has reduced and thickened slightly. Return the veal to the pan and heat through. Stir in the capers.

4 Lightly spray the sage leaves with olive oil spray, grill until crisp and scatter over the veal.

5 Drizzle vinegar over the tomatoes and season with pepper. Serve the veal on the cornmeal and tomatoes on the side. Serves 4

STAR INGREDIENT

CORNMEAL, or polenta in Italian, is made by crushing dried corn or maize. It varies in colour from white to bright yellow, and in texture from very fine to quite coarse. It is sold in supermarkets and health food stores. Cornmeal is a good source of carbohydrate, fibre, thiamin and iron, and a moderate source of protein and niacin.

Turkey Steaks with Balsamic Onions and Sweet Potato Mash

PREP TIME **40 minutes** COOKING TIME **30 minutes**

8 pickling onions (see tip),
   halved with the root intact
3 tablespoons balsamic vinegar
1 tablespoon brown sugar
4 (about 600g) turkey thigh steaks
canola cooking spray

750g orange sweet potato,
   peeled and chopped
3 tablespoons chopped fresh dill
1 1/2 tablespoons reduced fat sour cream

1 Put the pickling onions, vinegar, brown sugar and 3 tablespoons of water in a fry pan. Stir over a low heat until the sugar dissolves then cook, stirring occasionally, for 20 minutes or until the onions are soft and caramelised.

2 Trim the turkey steaks of any fat or sinew. Spray a large non stick fry pan with canola spray and heat until hot. Cook the steaks over a medium high heat for 5 minutes or until tender, turning once.

3 Cook the sweet potato in a large pot of boiling water until soft, drain and return to the pot. Add the dill and sour cream and mash until very smooth and creamy.

4 Place a mound of the sweet potato onto each plate, top with turkey steaks and balsamic onions. Serves 4

Thai Fish Burgers

PREP TIME **15 minutes** COOKING TIME **20 minutes**

500g redfish fillets, bones removed
2-3 tablespoons red curry paste
100g green beans, thinly sliced
4 kaffir lime leaves, finely shredded
8 Thai basil leaves, finely shredded
1 tablespoon soybean oil
4 wholegrain rolls, halved
100g watercress, washed

1 Lebanese cucumber, very thinly sliced
1 carrot, very thinly sliced

Dressing
1 tablespoon sweet chilli sauce
1 tablespoon lime juice
1/3 cup reduced fat natural yoghurt

1 Put the roughly chopped fish in a food processor, add the curry paste and process until smooth. Transfer the fish paste to a bowl and stir in the beans, kaffir lime leaves and basil and mix well to combine. Shape the mixture into four round, slightly flattened burgers.

2 Heat the oil in a large non stick fry pan, add the burgers and cook over a medium heat for 15 minutes, turning once, or until they are cooked through.

3 Toast the rolls and put watercress, cucumber and carrot on each base. Top each roll with a fish burger.

4 To make the dressing Put the sweet chilli sauce, lime juice and yoghurt in a bowl and whisk gently to combine.

5 Spoon the dressing over the burgers and cover with the toasted roll tops. Serves 4

NUTRIENTS per serve

Energy	1500kJ
Energy	358cal
Total fat	8.2g
Saturated fat	3.2g
Monounsaturated fat	2.0g
Polyunsaturated fat	1.7g
Protein	37.0g
Carbohydrate	33.0g
Fibre	4.3g
Sodium	391mg
Cholesterol	77mg

TIP

Pickling onions and pickled onions are not the same. Pickling onions are any variety of onion planted close together and harvested early so they are small. Pickled onions are the small pickling onions preserved in vinegar and spices.

NUTRIENTS per serve

Energy	1958kJ
Energy	468cal
Total fat	12.0g
Saturated fat	3.0g
Monounsaturated fat	2.6g
Polyunsaturated fat	4.9g
Protein	39.0g
Carbohydrate	51.0g
Fibre	8.4g
Sodium	997mg
Cholesterol	89mg

TIP

The popularity of Thai cuisine around the world makes it easy to find authentic fresh ingredients like lemon grass and kaffir limes in most supermarkets, Asian food stores and greengrocers.

Pork Fillet, Noodle and Sugar Snap Stir Fry

PREP TIME **10 minutes** COOKING TIME **15 minutes**

NUTRIENTS per serve

Energy	1047kJ
Energy	250cal
Total fat	7.0g
Saturated fat	0.9g
Monounsaturated fat	1.3g
Polyunsaturated fat	3.6g
Protein	29.0g
Carbohydrate	18.0g
Fibre	7.7g
Sodium	559mg
Cholesterol	43mg

TIP

Thick, dried rice stick noodles are fettuccine-like noodles used in stir fries, soups and salads. Packaged in bundles, they must be soaked in warm water and drained before using.

125g thick, dried rice stick noodles
1 tablespoon soybean oil
350g pork fillet, thinly sliced
4 spring onions, sliced
1 red capsicum, thinly sliced
200g sugar snap peas, trimmed
300g asparagus, cut into 4cm pieces
1 bunch choy sum, roughly chopped
3 tablespoons reduced salt soy sauce
3 tablespoons mirin
1 tablespoon sugar

1 Put the noodles in a large bowl, cover with boiling water and allow to stand for 10 minutes or until soft. Drain well.
2 Heat the oil in a wok until very hot, add the pork fillet slices and stir fry over a high heat until browned, just tender and cooked through. Remove and set aside.
3 Add the spring onions and capsicum to the wok with 2 tablespoons of water and cook until the capsicum is soft.
4 Add the remaining vegetables to the wok and stir fry until bright green and tender.
5 Return the pork to the wok along with the noodles. Stir in the combined soy, mirin and sugar and cook just until the sauce thickens slightly. Serves 4

STAR INGREDIENT
PORK cuts are often very lean thanks to new breeding techniques. Lean pork has slightly less fat than skinless chicken, lean lamb or lean beef. Spare ribs, bacon, salami and pork sausages are significantly higher in total and saturated fats. Look for lean cuts labelled with the Heart Foundation "Tick" of approval.

NUTRIENTS per serve

Energy	1914kJ
Energy	457cal
Total fat	17.0g
Saturated fat	7.3g
Monounsaturated fat	5.7g
Polyunsaturated fat	2.5g
Protein	41.0g
Carbohydrate	24.0g
Fibre	2.7g
Sodium	136mg
Cholesterol	99mg

TIP

Choose lean red meat and avoid cuts with lots of creamy marbling as they are very high in saturated fat. Trim all visible fat from meat cuts and allow the meat to rest after cooking: it helps keep all the rich juices in.

NUTRIENTS per serve

Energy	825kJ
Energy	197cal
Total fat	8.6g
Saturated fat	4.8g
Monounsaturated fat	2.5g
Polyunsaturated fat	0.5g
Protein	16.0g
Carbohydrate	14.0g
Fibre	6.0g
Sodium	703mg
Cholesterol	74mg

Beef with Green Peppercorn Sauce and Potatoes

PREP TIME 15 minutes COOKING TIME 15 minutes

12 small kipfler or baby potatoes, scrubbed
4 New York cut or sirloin steaks
2 teaspoons safflower oil
250ml white wine

125g can green peppercorns, drained and lightly bruised
1/3 cup reduced fat sour cream
12 chives, coarsely chopped

1 Steam or microwave the potatoes until tender, cut into thick slices and keep warm.
2 While the potatoes are cooking, trim the steaks of any excess fat or sinew. Heat the oil in a large fry pan, add the steaks and cook over a medium high heat until cooked to your liking, turning once. Remove and keep warm.
3 Add the white wine and peppercorns to the pan and boil over a high heat until reduced by half, scraping the bottom of the pan to remove any juices that may be stuck.
4 Stir in the sour cream and simmer until the sauce is thick enough to coat the back of a spoon.
5 Serve the steaks on top of the potatoes drizzled with peppercorn sauce and sprinkled with chives. Serves 4

Filo Pie with Silverbeet and Spicy Tomato

PREP TIME 30 minutes + standing COOKING TIME 50 minutes

olive oil cooking spray
100g bulgar or cracked wheat
1kg silverbeet, shredded
2 cloves garlic, crushed
6 spring onions, chopped
2 tablespoons chopped fresh dill
1/2 cup chopped fresh flat leaf parsley
3 tablespoons capers, drained and chopped

200g reduced fat ricotta cheese
250g reduced fat feta cheese
pinch nutmeg
2 eggs, lightly beaten
1/2 packet (about 187g) filo pastry
1/2 cup spicy tomato chutney
Greek salad and lemon wedges, to serve

1 Preheat oven to 200°C. Lightly spray a 20cm springform tin with olive oil spray.
2 Put the bulgar in a bowl, cover with 250ml boiling water and allow to stand for 10 minutes or until all the liquid has been absorbed.
3 Steam the silverbeet until it wilts, drain well and squeeze out any excess moisture. Chop coarsely and put in a bowl with the garlic, spring onions, herbs, capers, cheeses, nutmeg and eggs and mix to combine. Stir in the bulgar.
4 Lightly spray eight sheets of filo pastry with olive oil spray and layer the base and side of the springform tin with the pastry. Spoon the filling into the pastry lined tin and cover the filling with pastry.
5 Spray four extra sheets of filo with olive oil spray and cut into thin strips then scrunch up the filo and pile on top of the pie. Bake for 45 minutes or until the pastry is crisp and golden and the filling is set.
6 Serve wedges of the pie with the tomato chutney. Serves 6-8

Rigatoni with Pumpkin and Ginger Tofu

PREP TIME **25 minutes** COOKING TIME **25 minutes**

300g firm tofu
1 tablespoon fresh ginger, grated
1/2 teaspoon sesame oil
2 tablespoons reduced salt soy sauce
1 teaspoon brown sugar
1 tablespoon soybean oil
1 leek, washed and thinly sliced
500g pumpkin, peeled and chopped

1 cinnamon stick
250ml reduced salt vegetable stock
cracked black pepper to taste
1/4 cup fresh coriander, chopped
500g rigatoni (large dried pasta tubes)
2 tablespoons pine nuts, toasted
fresh coriander sprigs, to garnish

NUTRIENTS per serve

Energy	1784kJ
Energy	424cal
Total fat	10.6g
Saturated fat	1.2g
Monounsaturated fat	2.0g
Polyunsaturated fat	4.5g
Protein	16.0g
Carbohydrate	48.0g
Fibre	5.9g
Sodium	356mg
Cholesterol	0mg

1 Cut the tofu into thick slices and put in a shallow dish. Combine the ginger, sesame oil, soy and sugar and whisk until the sugar dissolves. Pour over the tofu and allow to marinate while preparing the other ingredients.

2 Heat the soybean oil in a medium pot, add the leek and cook over a medium heat until soft and golden. Add the pumpkin and cinnamon stick and cook until the pumpkin softens.

3 Add the stock, bring to the boil, cover and simmer until the pumpkin is tender. Transfer to a blender and blend until smooth. Season with cracked black pepper and stir the coriander through.

4 Cook the rigatoni in a large pot of rapidly boiling water until al dente (cooked, but still with a bite to it), drain and keep warm.

5 Drain the tofu and cook in a non stick fry pan over a medium heat until browned on both sides. Stir the pumpkin puree through the pasta. Top with caramelised tofu, pine nuts and coriander sprigs. Serves 4-6

STAR INGREDIENT
TOFU is made from soybeans. It is low in fat and an excellent source of protein. All soybean products contain phytoestrogens and soy protein which may protect against heart disease when used in a diet low in saturated fats and dietary cholesterol.

Pastitsio (pasta baked with meat sauce)

PREP TIME **20 minutes** COOKING TIME **1 hour 30 minutes**

NUTRIENTS per serve

Energy	1958kJ
Energy	468cal
Total fat	16.0g
Saturated fat	4.0g
Monounsaturated fat	5.7g
Polyunsaturated fat	4.5g
Protein	33.0g
Carbohydrate	46.0g
Fibre	4.0g
Sodium	297mg
Cholesterol	111mg

olive oil cooking spray
2 teaspoons olive oil
1 onion, chopped
2 cloves garlic, crushed
200g button mushrooms, sliced
750g lean beef mince
400g can chopped tomatoes
2 tablespoons reduced salt tomato paste
125ml red wine
125ml reduced salt beef stock
2 tablespoons chopped fresh
    flat leaf parsley

1 teaspoon sugar
350g ziti (long, fat, hollow dried pasta),
    or penne rigate
1 egg, lightly beaten
1 egg white, lightly beaten
pinch nutmeg

White sauce
1/3 cup polyunsaturated margarine
1/2 cup plain flour
750ml low or reduced fat milk
1 egg, lightly beaten

1 Preheat oven to 180°C. Spray a 35 x 25 cm ovenproof dish with cooking spray.
2 Heat the oil in a large fry pan, add the onion and garlic and cook over a medium heat for 3 minutes or until the onion is soft and golden. Add the mushrooms and cook for 5 minutes or until brown and tender. Add the mince and cook until browned, breaking up any lumps that form.
3 Stir in the tomatoes, tomato paste, red wine, stock and parsley and bring to the boil. Reduce the heat, cover and simmer for 20 minutes. Stir in the sugar.
4 Cook the pasta in a large pot of rapidly boiling water until al dente (cooked, but still with a bite to it), drain well and put on the base of the prepared dish. Pour over the combined egg, egg white and nutmeg.
5 To make the white sauce Melt the margarine in a small pot, add the flour and cook for 1 minute or until golden. Remove from the heat and add the milk. Stir until smooth, return to the heat and stir until the sauce boils and thickens. Simmer for 3 minutes. Remove from the heat and cool before stirring in the egg.
6 Add half the white sauce to the meat sauce. Spread the meat white sauce over the pasta, then top with plain white sauce. Bake for 50 minutes or until golden. Allow to stand for 10 minutes before slicing. Serves 6-8

Gnocchi with Spinach, Rocket and Basil Pesto

PREP TIME **15 minutes** COOKING TIME **15 minutes**

NUTRIENTS per serve

Energy	1505kJ
Energy	360cal
Total fat	21.2g
Saturated fat	2.9g
Monounsaturated fat	10.3g
Polyunsaturated fat	6.6g
Protein	10.3g
Carbohydrate	32.0g
Fibre	4.6g
Sodium	145mg
Cholesterol	5mg

500g fresh potato gnocchi
100g baby spinach leaves, washed
100g baby rocket leaves, washed
1 cup fresh basil leaves
2 cloves garlic

4 tablespoons pine nuts, toasted
1/4 cup grated parmesan cheese
2 tablespoons extra virgin olive oil
cracked black pepper to taste

1 Cook the gnocchi in a large pot of rapidly boiling water just until they float to the surface. Remove with a slotted spoon, drain well and keep warm.
2 Steam the spinach until it wilts, drain and squeeze out any excess moisture.
3 Put the spinach, rocket, basil, garlic, pine nuts and parmesan in a food processor and process until smooth. With the motor running, gradually add the olive oil and process to form a smooth paste.
4 Spoon the pesto over the cooked gnocchi and toss to coat. Season with cracked black pepper. Serves 4

Smoked Cod, Salmon and Potato Pie

PREP TIME **40 minutes** COOKING TIME **1 hour 10 minutes**

800g smoked cod
500ml low or reduced fat milk
200ml reduced salt fish stock
1 bay leaf
1 onion, studded with 3 cloves
50g polyunsaturated margarine
50g plain flour
100g smoked salmon, cut into thin strips

1 cup fresh or frozen peas
3 tablespoons fresh parsley, chopped
1 tablespoon lemon zest
1 tablespoon lemon juice
cracked black pepper
900g potatoes, chopped
30g reduced fat cheddar cheese, grated

NUTRIENTS per serve

Energy	1412kJ
Energy	336cal
Total fat	10.0g
Saturated fat	2.7g
Monounsaturated fat	3.1g
Polyunsaturated fat	3.8g
Protein	38.0g
Carbohydrate	23.4g
Fibre	3.4g
Sodium	870mg
Cholesterol	80mg

1 Preheat oven to 180°C. Put the smoked cod in a deep fry pan and add 400ml of the milk, the fish stock, bay leaf and the onion studded with cloves. Bring slowly to the boil. Reduce the heat, cover and simmer for 5 minutes or until the fish is tender. Remove the fish with a slotted spoon and set aside to cool.

2 Strain the poaching liquid into a jug. Melt the margarine in a small pot, add the flour and stir while cooking for 1 minute. Add the reserved poaching liquid and cook, stirring constantly, until the sauce boils and thickens. Simmer over a very low heat while preparing the fish.

3 Remove the skin from the cod and flake the flesh into large pieces. Mix the cod, salmon and peas together and put in the base of a 27cm long x 6cm deep ceramic baking dish. Add the parsley, capers, zest and juice to the sauce and season with freshly ground black pepper. Pour the sauce over the fish mixture. Chill.

4 Put the potatoes in a medium pot, cover with water and simmer for 20-25 minutes or until tender. Drain well. Warm the remaining 100ml milk. Using an electric hand beater whip the potatoes, gradually adding the milk until the mixture is soft and smooth. Season with pepper.

5 Spread the potato over the top of the fish to completely cover. Use a fork to make rough lines in the potato then sprinkle with cheese. Bake for 30 minutes. Serve with a crisp green salad or steamed baby beans. Serves 4-6

TIP

Marine omega-3 fats are the polyunsaturated fatty acids found mainly in fish and some shellfish. Marine omega-3 fats are valued for their ability to reduce the risk of heart attack, prevent irregular heartbeats (arrhythmia) and reduce blood triglyceride levels.

Individual Beef and Red Wine Pies

PREP TIME **30 minutes + cooling** COOKING TIME **2 hours 25 minutes**

2 teaspoons peanut oil
1 large onion, chopped
2 cloves garlic, crushed
1 kg beef chuck steak
    trimmed of all fat and cubed
2 tablespoons plain flour
2 tablespoons reduced salt tomato paste
375ml red wine

375ml reduced salt beef stock
2 carrots, thinly sliced
200g Swiss brown mushrooms, quartered
2 tablespoons fresh thyme, chopped
2 tablespoons fresh parsley, chopped
2 sheets canola puff pastry, defrosted
4 sprigs thyme
1 tablespoon low or reduced fat milk

1 Preheat the oven to 200°C. You will need 6 x 2 cup capacity ovenproof pie dishes.
2 Heat the oil in a large pot, add the onion and cook over a medium heat for 5 minutes or until golden. Add the garlic and the beef and cook for 5 minutes until the beef is browned.
3 Add the flour and tomato paste and cook for a further 2 minutes, stirring constantly. Stir in the red wine and stock and bring to the boil. Add the carrots, mushrooms and chopped thyme. Reduce the heat, cover and simmer for about 1 hour then remove the lid and cook for a further 45 minutes until the beef is tender and the sauce is reduced and thickened. Stir through the parsley, transfer to a bowl and allow the filling to cool completely.
4 Using the top of a pie dish as a guide, cut 6 circles from the pastry, about 2cm larger than the dish. Spoon the cooled filling into the dishes. Brush the edges of each pastry circle with a little water then cover the dishes (damp side down); pressing the pastry to the side of the dish to seal. Cut a small cross in the top of each pie, insert a sprig of thyme and lightly brush with milk.
5 Bake for 20-25 minutes or until the pastry is crisp and golden and the filling is hot. Serve the pies with mashed potato and steamed beans. Makes 6

Asian Marinated Chicken Drumsticks

PREP TIME **20 minutes + marinating** COOKING TIME **40 minutes**

12 large chicken drumsticks
1/2 cup hoisin sauce
3 tablespoons golden syrup
1 tablespoon lemon juice
1 tablespoon sunflower oil

2 cloves garlic, crushed
4 spring onions, thinly sliced on the
    diagonal
4 baby bok choy, halved
steamed rice, to serve

1 Remove the skin from the drumsticks and discard any excess fat. Make 2 or 3 deep slashes in the fleshy part of the chicken.
2 Put the hoisin, golden syrup, lemon juice, oil and garlic in a large bowl and mix to combine. Coat the drumsticks with the mixture, cover and marinate in the refrigerator for 1 hour or overnight if you have time.
3 Preheat oven to 200°C. Line a baking tray with non stick paper. Put the drumsticks on the paper and roast for 40 minutes or until tender and the juices run clear when tested with a skewer. Sprinkle the drumsticks with the spring onions.
4 Steam the bok choy in a bamboo steamer over a wok of simmering water, making sure the base of the steamer does not touch the water. Serve the chicken on top of the steamed bok choy with steamed rice on the side. Serves 4

NUTRIENTS per serve

Energy	1359kJ
Energy	325cal
Total fat	8.6g
Saturated fat	3.4g
Monounsaturated fat	3.8g
Polyunsaturated fat	1.2g
Protein	38.0g
Carbohydrate	13.0g
Fibre	2.4g
Sodium	397mg
Cholesterol	112mg

TIP
Everyone loves a hearty meat pie in winter. But many commercial meat pies are high in (mainly) saturated fats, cholesterol and salt. Home made meat pies, made with lean beef and canola puff pastry, are a healthier alternative.

NUTRIENTS per serve

Energy	1817kJ
Energy	434cal
Total fat	17.0g
Saturated fat	3.7g
Monounsaturated fat	6.2g
Polyunsaturated fat	4.9g
Protein	42.0g
Carbohydrate	29.0g
Fibre	7.9g
Sodium	690mg
Cholesterol	154mg

Seafood Risotto

PREP TIME **40 minutes** COOKING TIME **40 minutes**

400g green prawns
250ml white wine
1 litre reduced salt fish stock
250ml water
pinch saffron
2 teaspoons sunflower oil
2 cloves garlic, crushed
150g squid tubes, cut into rings

150g firm, skinless, boneless white fish
   fillets, cut into 2cm cubes
150g scallops
1 onion, thinly sliced
2 cups arborio (risotto) rice
1 tablespoon chopped fresh chives
1 tablespoon lemon juice
cracked black pepper to serve

1 Peel and devein the prawns, leaving the tails intact. Put the shells in a small pot with wine, stock and water and bring to the boil. Reduce the heat and simmer for 15 minutes over a high heat then drain and discard the shells. Return the liquid and saffron to the pot and keep at simmering point.

2 Heat the oil in a large, deep fry pan, add the garlic, prawns, squid, fish and scallops in separate batches and cook over a high heat just until they change colour. Remove from the pan and set aside.

3 Add the onion to the pan and cook until golden, add the rice and cook, stirring constantly, until the rice starts to whiten after a couple of minutes.

4 Stir in the saffron stock one ladle at a time and cook, stirring constantly, until most of the liquid has been absorbed. Continue adding the stock a ladle at a time until all the stock is absorbed and the rice is tender. Beat the rice with a wooden spoon until it is a creamy texture.

5 Stir in the cooked seafood and chives. Season with lemon juice and a little cracked black pepper. Serves 4

NUTRIENTS per serve

Energy	2916kJ
Energy	697cal
Total fat	5.5g
Saturated fat	1.1g
Monounsaturated fat	1.3g
Polyunsaturated fat	2.2g
Protein	48.0g
Carbohydrate	102.0g
Fibre	3.6g
Sodium	992mg
Cholesterol	262mg

TIP

It only takes a few minutes to cook fresh fish and seafood. As soon as the flesh turns opaque and flakes easily it is cooked. Overcooked fish will have less moisture and flavour, so keep an eye on it.

STAR INGREDIENT

PRAWNS have a higher cholesterol content than most other seafood. Yet the most positive features of prawns are often overlooked: they contain almost no saturated fat and are rich in protein. When included as part of a low saturated fat eating pattern, they are fine in moderation unless indicated otherwise by your doctor or dietitian.

Vegetables and Side Dishes

As well as adding great flavour and colour to your meals, vegetables and side dishes can also provide essential nutrients for your, and your family's, heart health. With speed and simplicity in mind we've made it easy to enjoy healthy eating.

NUTRIENTS per serve

Energy	288kJ
Energy	69cal
Total fat	3.7g
Saturated fat	0.3g
Monounsaturated fat	0.8g
Polyunsaturated fat	2.0g
Protein	4.4g
Carbohydrate	4.4g
Fibre	3.3g
Sodium	171mg
Cholesterol	0mg

STAR INGREDIENT

LENTILS are a small legume related to the pea and may be green, brown or bright orange-red. They are low in fat, contain no cholesterol, are high in some B vitamins and provide an excellent source of vegetable protein for non-meat eaters.

NUTRIENTS per serve

Energy	592kJ
Energy	141cal
Total fat	4.3g
Saturated fat	0.4g
Monounsaturated fat	0.6g
Polyunsaturated fat	2.6g
Protein	12.0g
Carbohydrate	13.0g
Fibre	8.0g
Sodium	329mg
Cholesterol	0mg

Marinated Mushroom and Capsicum

PREP TIME **30 minutes + marinating** COOKING TIME **5 minutes**

1 red capsicum
1 yellow capsicum
1 green capsicum
4 spring onions, sliced
500g button mushrooms, halved
2 cloves garlic, crushed

1 tablespoon wholegrain honey mustard
125ml Italian salad dressing
2 tablespoons chopped fresh
   flat leaf parsley
1 tablespoon fresh thyme, chopped

1 Cut the capsicums in half and remove the seeds and membranes. Cook the capsicum halves on a baking tray under a hot grill until the skin blisters and blackens. Transfer them to a plastic bag and allow to cool. Peel away the skin and discard, then cut the flesh into thin strips.
2 Put the capsicum strips, spring onions and mushrooms in a bowl and toss to combine.
3 Whisk together the garlic, mustard, salad dressing and herbs and pour over the mushrooms. Stir well to ensure the capsicum and mushrooms are coated with dressing, then cover and allow to marinate for up to 4 hours. Serves 4-6

Puy Lentils with Spring Vegetables

PREP TIME **20 minutes** COOKING TIME **30 minutes**

1 bunch asparagus, cut into 3cm lengths
300g broccoli, cut into florets
100g sugar snap peas, trimmed
1 cup Puy (small French) lentils
250ml reduced salt vegetable stock
1 tablespoon safflower oil

1 clove garlic, crushed
1 tablespoon honey mustard
1 tablespoon lemon juice
3 tablespoons fresh basil, finely shredded
100g baby spinach leaves, washed
cracked black pepper to taste

1 Steam or blanch the asparagus, broccoli and sugar snap peas just until tender and still bright green. Rinse under cold water and drain. Set aside.
2 Put the lentils in a large pot, add the stock and add 250ml of water and bring to the boil. Reduce the heat and simmer for 20 minutes or until the lentils are tender. Do not overcook or they will be mushy. Drain, reserving 60ml of the stock.
3 Return the lentils to the pot, add the oil, garlic, mustard, lemon juice, reserved stock and steamed or blanched vegetables. Cook over a low heat for 2 minutes or just until warmed through.
4 Remove from the heat and stir through the basil and spinach. Season with cracked black pepper. Serves 4-6

Roasted Vegetables with Sesame Seeds

PREP TIME **20 minutes**   COOKING TIME **30 minutes**

250g pumpkin
300g orange sweet potato
1 large red capsicum
500g baby red or new potatoes
8 small or pickling onions, peeled
1 tablespoon olive oil

2 cloves garlic, crushed
1 tablespoon honey
2 tablespoons sesame seeds, toasted
1 tablespoon fresh rosemary sprigs
cracked black pepper

1 Preheat the oven to 200°C.
2 Peel the pumpkin and cut it into large pieces. Cut the sweet potato into large pieces. Remove the seeds and membrane from the capsicum and cut into large pieces. Toss the prepared vegetables together with the potatoes and onions in a large baking dish.
3 Drizzle with the combined oil, garlic and honey and toss to combine. Bake for 30 minutes or until the vegetables are tender.
4 Remove from the oven, and sprinkle with sesame seeds and rosemary sprigs. Season with cracked black pepper. Serves 4-6

NUTRIENTS per serve

Energy	772kJ
Energy	184cal
Total fat	5.0g
Saturated fat	0.8g
Monounsaturated fat	2.9g
Polyunsaturated fat	0.9g
Protein	4.7g
Carbohydrate	30.0g
Fibre	3.8g
Sodium	200mg
Cholesterol	0mg

TIP
Generally speaking, vegetables that are served just cooked or slightly undercooked retain a higher vitamin content than overcooked vegetables.

TIP
Where possible, leave vegetables that have edible skins (such as potatoes, parsnips or carrots) unpeeled. This will increase the amount of dietary fibre in meals. Just remember to wash or scrub unpeeled vegetables thoroughly before cooking with the skins on.

Creamy Potato Gratin

PREP TIME 15 minutes COOKING TIME 45 minutes

750g waxy potatoes (desiree or sebago)
1 onion, thinly sliced
375ml reduced fat evaporated milk

125ml reduced salt chicken stock
1/2 cup grated reduced fat cheddar cheese

1 Preheat the oven to 180°C. Peel the potatoes and cut into thin slices. Layer the potato and onion in a 6 cup capacity ovenproof dish.
2 Whisk together the evaporated milk, chicken stock and half the cheese. Pour over the layered potato.
3 Sprinkle with the grated cheese and bake, covered, for 30 minutes then uncovered for 15 minutes or until the potato is tender and the cheese is golden. Serves 4-6

TIP
When highly flavoured ingredients such as lemon zest, vinegar or herbs are used in recipes, the need for salt will be significantly lower.

NUTRIENTS per serve

Energy	1018kJ
Energy	243cal
Total fat	6.6g
Saturated fat	4.0g
Monounsaturated fat	1.8g
Polyunsaturated fat	0.2g
Protein	15.0g
Carbohydrate	30.0g
Fibre	3.0g
Sodium	291mg
Cholesterol	21mg

Roasted Tomato, Basil and Feta

PREP TIME 5 minutes COOKING TIME 20 minutes

16 small vine ripened tomatoes,
   still attached to the vine
100g reduced fat feta cheese
1/2 teaspoon lemon zest

2 tablespoons fresh basil leaves,
   finely shredded
cracked black pepper to taste
1 tablespoon balsamic vinegar

1 Preheat the oven to 180°C.
2 Cut the vine ripened tomatoes in groups of four. Carefully slice off the tops making sure the stems remain attached. Carefully remove the pulp with a teaspoon and discard it.
3 Combine the feta, lemon, basil and a little cracked black pepper. Stuff the filling equally into the tomatoes.
4 Put the tops back onto the tomatoes. Insert toothpicks through the top of the tomatoes to hold them together. Put the tomatoes on a non stick baking tray.
Bake for 15-20 minutes or until the feta starts to melt and the skins soften.
Drizzle with balsamic vinegar just before serving. Serves 4

NUTRIENTS per serve

Energy	738kJ
Energy	176cal
Total fat	8.9g
Saturated fat	3.0g
Monounsaturated fat	4.5g
Polyunsaturated fat	0.6g
Protein	12.0g
Carbohydrate	11.0g
Fibre	6.8g
Sodium	309mg
Cholesterol	15mg

Chargrilled Asparagus and Leeks

PREP TIME 10 minutes   COOKING TIME 10 minutes

2 small leeks
2 bunches asparagus
olive oil cooking spray
300g can butter beans, drained

2 tablespoons extra virgin olive oil
4 tablespoons flaked almonds
1/4 cup shaved parmesan
2 tablespoons balsamic vinegar

NUTRIENTS per serve

Energy	824kJ
Energy	197cal
Total fat	17.0g
Saturated fat	3.3g
Monounsaturated fat	11.0g
Polyunsaturated fat	2.2g
Protein	7.9g
Carbohydrate	3.6g
Fibre	4.6g
Sodium	121mg
Cholesterol	7.42mg

1 Cut the leeks in half lengthwise, then into quarters and wash thoroughly. Trim any woody ends from the asparagus.

2 Spray a chargrill or barbecue with olive oil spray and heat until very hot. Cook the leek and asparagus over a medium high heat until tender. Transfer to a serving plate.

3 Toss the butter beans with 1 tablespoon of the oil and cook over a medium heat for 5 minutes or until heated through.

4 Spoon the butter beans over the asparagus and leeks. Combine the almonds and parmesan in a small bowl, sprinkle over the beans and drizzle with the combined balsamic and remaining oil. Serves 4

STAR INGREDIENT
ASPARAGUS is an excellent source of folic acid and supplies lots of vitamin C. When buying asparagus look for tips that are tightly compressed and fresh looking, and firm stalks. To prepare asparagus for cooking snap off the coarse base, rinse under cold water and cook as directed.

Mixed Beans with Pine Nuts and Parmesan

PREP TIME 10 minutes   COOKING TIME 10 minutes

250g yellow beans, trimmed
200g green beans, trimmed
2 tablespoons red wine vinegar
1 teaspoon honey
1 clove garlic, crushed

2 tablespoons fresh mint, finely sliced
1 tablespoon mustard seed oil
2 tablespoons pine nuts, toasted
2 tablespoons shaved parmesan
cracked black pepper to taste

1 Steam or microwave the beans until tender. Do not overcook or they will lose their colour. Drain well.
2 Whisk together the red wine vinegar, honey, garlic, mint and mustard seed oil in a small jug.
3 Pour the dressing over the beans and top with the toasted pine nuts, parmesan and cracked black pepper. Serves 4

To shave parmesan, run a vegetable peeler down one side of a triangle of parmesan cheese to make delicate, thin strips.

NUTRIENTS per serve

Energy	612kJ
Energy	146cal
Total fat	12.0g
Saturated fat	1.8g
Monounsaturated fat	2.8g
Polyunsaturated fat	6.5g
Protein	5.4g
Carbohydrate	4.5g
Fibre	3.6g
Sodium	76mg
Cholesterol	4.75mg

TIP
Antioxidants protect against free radicals in the body. Most fruits, vegetables, wholegrain cereals and cereal products are rich in antioxidants, so eating a variety of these every day is beneficial.

Individual Macaroni, Broccolini and Cauliflower Cheese

PREP TIME 20 minutes   COOKING TIME 30 minutes

50g macaroni
250g cauliflower, cut into florets
250g broccolini or broccoli, cut into florets
20g canola spread

1 tablespoon plain flour
pinch saffron
pinch nutmeg
250ml reduced fat evaporated milk
1/3 cup grated reduced fat cheddar cheese

1 Preheat oven to 200°C. Lightly grease four 250ml ramekins (ceramic ovenproof dishes).
2 Cook the macaroni in a large pot of rapidly boiling water until al dente (cooked, but still with a bite to it). Drain well and set aside.
3 Steam or microwave the cauliflower and broccolini or broccoli separately until tender. Rinse under cold water and drain well.
4 Heat the canola spread in a small pot, add the flour, saffron and nutmeg and cook, stirring constantly, until bubbling. Remove from the heat and gradually stir in the milk.
5 Return the pot to the heat and bring to the boil, stirring constantly until the sauce boils and thickens. Reduce the heat and simmer for 5 minutes.
6 Put the macaroni in the base of the ramekins, top with the combined cauliflower and broccolini and pour over the sauce. Sprinkle with cheese. Bake for 15 minutes or until the sauce is golden and bubbling. Serves 4

This recipe can also be made in a single large ovenproof dish.

NUTRIENTS per serve

Energy	764kJ
Energy	182cal
Total fat	5.7g
Saturated fat	2.5g
Monounsaturated fat	1.5g
Polyunsaturated fat	1.1g
Protein	13.0g
Carbohydrate	19.0g
Fibre	4.4g
Sodium	156mg
Cholesterol	11mg

Spicy Chickpea and Spinach Salad

PREP TIME 15 minutes COOKING TIME 10 minutes

2 tablespoons olive oil
2 cloves garlic, crushed
1 red onion, thinly sliced
pinch dried red chilli flakes
1 carrot, finely chopped
1 red capsicum, finely chopped
300g can chickpeas, rinsed and drained

150g baby spinach leaves, washed
100g semi-dried tomatoes, chopped
2 tablespoons lemon juice
125ml white wine
3 tablespoons chopped fresh herbs
   (parsley, oregano, chives)

1 Heat the oil in a large fry pan, add the garlic, onion and chilli flakes and cook over a medium heat until the onion is soft.
2 Add the carrot and capsicum and cook until tender. Stir in the chickpeas, spinach, semi-dried tomatoes, lemon juice and wine and bring to the boil. Reduce the heat and simmer for 2 minutes or until the spinach wilts.
3 Remove from the heat, stir through the herbs and serve warm or cold.
Serves 4-6

NUTRIENTS per serve

Energy	565kJ
Energy	135cal
Total fat	7.6g
Saturated fat	1.1g
Monounsaturated fat	4.7g
Polyunsaturated fat	1.1g
Protein	4.9g
Carbohydrate	9.9g
Fibre	4.4g
Sodium	144mg
Cholesterol	0mg

TIP

Be adventurous! Try a wide variety of vegetables and at least two serves of fruit each day, and add even more dietary fibre to your meals by using dried and canned lentils, split peas, chickpeas or baked beans.

Fragrant Dhal (Indian lentils)

PREP TIME 15 minutes COOKING TIME 30 minutes

200g red lentils
2 tablespoons safflower oil
1 tablespoon canola spread
1 onion, finely sliced
2 fresh green chillies, finely chopped

1 teaspoon brown mustard seeds
1/2 teaspoon ground turmeric
6 fresh curry leaves
1 tablespoon fresh coriander, chopped

1 Simmer the lentils in 750ml boiling water for about 20 minutes or until soft. Stir a couple of times during cooking to make sure they do not stick to the bottom of the pot. Do not drain.
2 Heat the oil and canola spread in a large fry pan, add the onion and chillies and cook over a medium heat until the onion is soft and golden.
3 Add the mustard seeds, turmeric and curry leaves and cook until the mustard seeds begin to pop.
4 Stir in the undrained lentils and fresh coriander and cook over a medium heat for a couple of minutes or until the mixture is heated through and slightly creamy.
Serve alone or with microwave poppadoms. Serves 4

NUTRIENTS per serve

Energy	909kJ
Energy	217cal
Total fat	10.0g
Saturated fat	1.2g
Monounsaturated fat	1.6g
Polyunsaturated fat	6.6g
Protein	13.0g
Carbohydrate	19.0g
Fibre	7.3g
Sodium	18mg
Cholesterol	0mg

Baby Eggplant with Ginger and Sweet Soy

PREP TIME 15 minutes COOKING TIME 15 minutes

8 slender eggplant
canola cooking spray
3 cloves garlic, crushed
1 tablespoon grated fresh ginger
1 teaspoon cumin seeds

pinch chilli powder
1 tablespoon kecap manis
  (sweet soy sauce)
2 tablespoons lemon juice
1/4 cup Thai basil leaves

1 Cut the eggplants in half, leaving the stems attached. Spray the cut sides lightly with the canola spray.
2 Heat a large non stick fry pan over a medium heat and add the eggplants, cut side down, and cook until they start to soften and turn golden. Remove.
3 Add the garlic, ginger, cumin, chilli powder and 1 tablespoon water to the pan and cook until the garlic is soft.
4 Stir in the kecap manis, lemon juice and 125ml water and bring to a low simmer. Return the eggplant to the pan and cook for 10 minutes or until soft and most of the liquid has been absorbed. Transfer to serving plates and top with Thai basil leaves. Serves 4-6

Serve warm or cold as an accompaniment to vegetable or lamb dishes.

NUTRIENTS per serve

Energy	163kJ
Energy	39cal
Total fat	0.7g
Saturated fat	0g
Monounsaturated fat	0g
Polyunsaturated fat	0g
Protein	2.4g
Carbohydrate	5.6g
Fibre	4.8g
Sodium	200mg
Cholesterol	0mg

TIP

Kecap manis (or ketjap manis) is a thick, sweet Indonesian soy sauce. Store it in a cool dry place and refrigerate after opening. If it is unavailable, use soy sauce sweetened with a little brown sugar.

Asian Greens with Sweet Soy and Sesame Dressing

PREP TIME 5 minutes COOKING TIME 5 minutes

500g baby bok choy
500g Chinese broccoli
300g water spinach
1/2 teaspoon sesame oil
1 tablespoon oyster sauce

1 tablespoon kecap manis
  (sweet soy sauce)
1 tablespoon rice vinegar
1 tablespoon sesame seeds, toasted

1 Cut the bok choy, Chinese broccoli and water spinach into 20cm lengths. Wash, drain and put in a large bamboo steamer lined with baking paper. Cook over a wok of simmering water, making sure the base of the steamer does not come in contact with the water, for 5 minutes or until bright green and tender.
2 Whisk together the sesame oil, oyster sauce, kecap manis and rice vinegar in a jug.
3 Neatly pile the vegetables onto a serving plate and drizzle with the sauce. Sprinkle with sesame seeds and serve. Serves 4-6

NUTRIENTS per serve

Energy	314kJ
Energy	75cal
Total fat	2.6g
Saturated fat	0.3g
Monounsaturated fat	0.7g
Polyunsaturated fat	0.9g
Protein	10.0g
Carbohydrate	2.3g
Fibre	8.6g
Sodium	417mg
Cholesterol	0mg

Dessert

You're in for a great surprise. Just turn the page to find out that maintaining a healthy heart doesn't always mean missing out on sweet treats. We've based our delicious desserts on plenty of fresh fruit so you can indulge in great looking, great tasting treats with family and friends.

Creamed Rice with Honey Macadamia Pears

PREP TIME **20 minutes** COOKING TIME **35 minutes**

1 cup arborio (risotto) rice
500ml low or reduced fat milk
2 tablespoons soft brown sugar
1 vanilla bean, cut in half lengthwise
2 tablespoons custard powder
3 tablespoons honey

1 teaspoon ground cinnamon
2 large beurre bosc pears, peeled and cut into thick lengthwise slices
4 tablespoons macadamia nuts, roasted and chopped

1 Put the rice, 750ml water, milk and sugar in a pot. Scrape in the seeds from the vanilla bean, add the bean itself and bring to the boil. Reduce the heat and simmer for 20 minutes, stirring regularly, or until the rice is tender.
2 Blend the custard powder with 2 tablespoons water and stir through the rice mixture. Continue stirring until the mixture boils, then simmer for 2 minutes until the mixture thickens. Remove from the heat, cover the surface of the rice mixture with plastic wrap and allow to stand while preparing the pears.
3 Gently heat the honey and cinnamon in a shallow fry pan, add the pear slices in batches and cook over a medium heat until they brown and soften slightly. Remove from the heat.
4 Remove the vanilla bean and spoon the creamed rice into bowls. Stand pear slices upright at the edge of each bowl. Sprinkle with chopped macadamias. Serves 4

NUTRIENTS per serve

Energy	1955kJ
Energy	467cal
Total fat	11.0g
Saturated fat	1.8g
Monounsaturated fat	8.4g
Polyunsaturated fat	0.2g
Protein	9.7g
Carbohydrate	84.0g
Fibre	3.6g
Sodium	75mg
Cholesterol	5.03mg

TIP
When baking, substitute polyunsaturated margarine for butter, lard, ghee, copha, palm oil or block cooking margarine: all of these are high in saturated fats.

Chocolate Raspberry Brownies

PREP TIME **20 minutes** COOKING TIME **35 minutes**

1/2 cup plain flour
1/2 cup self-raising flour
1 teaspoon bicarbonate of soda
3/4 cup cocoa
2 eggs, lightly beaten
1 1/4 cups caster sugar
1 teaspoon vanilla essence

1 1/2 tablespoons sunflower oil
200g thick reduced fat vanilla yoghurt
120g apple puree
200g fresh or frozen raspberries
icing sugar, to dust
fresh berries, to serve

1 Preheat oven to 180°C. Grease and line the base and sides of a 30cm x 20cm tin with baking paper.
2 Sift the flours, bicarbonate of soda and cocoa into a large bowl and make a well in the centre.
3 Whisk together the eggs, sugar, vanilla, oil and yoghurt in a large jug. Add to the flours and mix until smooth. Fold through the apple puree and raspberries.
4 Spoon the mixture into the prepared tin and bake for 30 minutes or until a skewer comes out clean when inserted in the centre. Allow to cool for 5 minutes in the tin before turning out onto a wire rack to cool completely.
5 Cut into squares and dust with icing sugar. Serve with extra fresh berries and reduced fat ice-cream. Makes 16

NUTRIENTS per serve

Energy	675kJ
Energy	161cal
Total fat	4.4g
Saturated fat	1.5g
Monounsaturated fat	1.3g
Polyunsaturated fat	1.2g
Protein	3.4g
Carbohydrate	26.0g
Fibre	1.6g
Sodium	73mg
Cholesterol	24mg

Christmas Cake with Frosted Fruit

PREP TIME **30 minutes + overnight standing**   COOKING TIME **3 hours 30 minutes**

1kg mixed dried fruit
150g glacé apricots, chopped
150g glacé cherries, chopped
50g glacé ginger, chopped
250ml brandy
1 cup soft brown sugar
2 tablespoons safflower oil
3 egg whites, lightly beaten
1 teaspoon vanilla essence
100g blanched almonds, roughly chopped
1 tablespoon lime ginger marmalade
60ml orange juice
2 cups plain flour

1/2 cup self-raising flour
2 teaspoons mixed spice

Icing
1 egg white
2 teaspoons lemon juice
1/2 cup pure icing sugar, sifted

Frosted fruit
500g mixed fresh fruit (eg berries, cherries, grapes)
2 egg whites, lightly beaten
2 cups caster sugar

1 Put the mixed dried fruit, apricots, cherries and ginger in a large bowl and mix. Pour over the brandy, cover and allow to stand overnight.
2 Preheat the oven to 150°C. Grease and line the base and sides of a 20cm round or 23cm square cake tin with 2 layers of baking paper.
3 Put the sugar, oil, egg whites and vanilla in a bowl and beat until smooth. Add the almonds, marmalade and orange juice. Stir through the dried fruit mixture.
4 Sift the flours and spice into a bowl, then fold in the fruit. Spoon the mixture into the prepared tin, then tap the tin on the bench to remove any air bubbles. Smooth the surface of the cake with damp hands. Wrap several layers of newspaper around the outside of the tin and secure with string to stop the outside of the cake from burning. Bake on the middle shelf of the oven for 3-3 1/2 hours or until a skewer comes out clean when inserted in the centre. Loosely cover the top of the cake with baking paper if it starts to darken too much during cooking. Cool completely then cover with icing and top with frosted fruit.
5 To make the icing Blend all ingredients together until smooth.
6 To make the frosted fruit Brush the fruit with egg white, roll in caster sugar and allow to dry. Serves 30

STAR INGREDIENT
MIXED DRIED FRUIT are high in dietary fibre and low in saturated fats. They are great to keep in the cupboard for a healthy snack or to add to sweet and savoury recipes.

Chocolate Mousse with Fresh Berries

PREP TIME **20 minutes** + chilling COOKING TIME **15 minutes**

175g dark chocolate, chopped
2 teaspoons powdered gelatin
100g reduced fat ricotta
250ml reduced fat vanilla custard

4 egg whites
300g mixed fresh berries
   (strawberries, raspberries, blueberries)

1 Put the chocolate in an ovenproof bowl over a pot of simmering water, making sure the base of the bowl does not come in contact with the water and that no water touches the chocolate. Stir over a low heat until the chocolate melts then set aside to cool slightly.
2 Put the gelatin and 60ml water into a small pot and stir over a low heat until the gelatin dissolves and the liquid is clear. Remove from the heat and allow to cool slightly.
3 Beat the ricotta and custard together until smooth. Press through a sieve to remove any lumps.
4 Beat the egg whites until stiff peaks form. Fold through the ricotta mix.
5 Fold the gelatin and chocolate into the ricotta mix. Spoon the mousse into six 125ml capacity ramekins or mugs, cover and refrigerate for 1 hour or until set. Serve with mixed fresh berries. Serves 6

NUTRIENTS per serve

Energy	963kJ
Energy	230cal
Total fat	10.0g
Saturated fat	5.6g
Monounsaturated fat	3.3g
Polyunsaturated fat	0.8g
Protein	8.3g
Carbohydrate	26.0g
Fibre	1.5g
Sodium	120mg
Cholesterol	10mg

STAR INGREDIENT
ALMOND MEAL is simply blanched, ground almonds. Almonds contain more calcium than any other nut and are a good source of monounsaturated fat, dietary fibre, vitamin E, iron, zinc, potassium and riboflavin (a B vitamin).

NUTRIENTS per serve

Energy	888kJ
Energy	212cal
Total fat	8.0g
Saturated fat	1.4g
Monounsaturated fat	3.4g
Polyunsaturated fat	2.6g
Protein	3.4g
Carbohydrate	33.0g
Fibre	1.0g
Sodium	30mg
Cholesterol	0mg

Almond, Blueberry and Marshmallow Friands

PREP TIME **15 minutes** COOKING TIME **20 minutes**

1 1/2 cups icing sugar
1 cup plain flour
1 teaspoon mixed spice
1 cup almond meal
5 egg whites

140g apple puree
2 tablespoons macadamia oil
150g fresh or frozen blueberries
1 cup white marshmallows,
   roughly chopped

1 Preheat oven to 200°C. Lightly grease and line the base of ten friand tins or twelve 125ml capacity muffin tins.
2 Sift the icing sugar, flour and mixed spice into a large bowl and stir in the almond meal.
3 Whisk the egg whites until foamy, add to the dry ingredients and mix to combine. Stir in the combined apple puree and macadamia oil.
4 Fold in the blueberries and marshmallows. Spoon the mixture into the prepared tins and bake for 20 minutes or until a skewer inserted in the centre comes out clean.
5 Allow to stand for 5 minutes in their tins before turning out onto a wire rack to cool completely. Serve for morning or afternoon tea or coffee. Makes 10

Ricotta Torte with Fruit Compote

PREP TIME **40 minutes + chilling** COOKING TIME **5 minutes**

canola cooking spray
150g reduced fat plain (sweet) biscuits
30g pecan nuts, toasted
50g polyunsaturated spread
    or margarine, melted
1 1/2 teaspoons powdered gelatin
zest and juice of 1 small orange
zest and juice of 1 small lemon
350g reduced fat ricotta cheese,
    well drained
1/4 cup caster sugar

250g reduced fat sour cream
2 eggs, separated

Fruit compote
75g dried figs
75g pitted prunes
75g dried apricots
75g dried cherries
25ml good quality marsala
80ml orange juice
zest of 1 orange

1 Spray a 20cm springform tin with canola spray and line the base with baking paper. Process the biscuits and nuts to fine crumbs. Add the margarine and process for a few seconds to combine. Press firmly into the base of the tin. Chill for 30 minutes.
2 Dissolve the gelatin in 1/4 cup boiling water. Put the combined juices (but not the zest) in a small pot and heat gently. Add the gelatin. Remove from the heat and stir to dissolve the gelatin.
3 Beat the ricotta, sugar, sour cream, egg yolks and zest with an electric beater, then gradually pour in the gelatin mixture and beat slowly to combine.
4 Whisk the egg whites until stiff peaks form, fold 2 or 3 tablespoons of the egg whites into the ricotta mixture to lighten, then fold through the remaining whites, trying not to deflate the mix. Pour over the biscuit base, cover and chill for at least 3 hours. Slice into 10 portions.
5 To make the fruit compote Put the figs, prunes, apricots and cherries in a bowl and add the marsala, orange juice and zest. Macerate in the refrigerator overnight. Serve the torte with fruit compote. Serves 10

NUTRIENTS per serve

Energy	1149kJ
Energy	274cal
Total fat	15.0g
Saturated fat	6.4g
Monounsaturated fat	5.0g
Polyunsaturated fat	2.9g
Protein	5.56g
Carbohydrate	29.5g
Fibre	3.0g
Sodium	138mg
Cholesterol	67mg

STAR INGREDIENT
RICOTTA is a moist and delicate cheese made from milk whey. It is an ideal substitute for cream cheese in desserts when a reduced fat content is required and is also delicious in savoury dishes. Reduced fat ricotta contains about 5% fat and has less salt than regular cheese.

Boiled Orange, Lime and Almond Cake

PREP TIME **10 minutes** COOKING TIME **3 hours**

2 navel oranges and 4 thin skinned limes,
   (about 375g total weight)
canola cooking spray
3 eggs
4 egg whites

1 1/2 cups sugar
1 teaspoon baking powder
225g almond meal
reduced fat ice-cream or yoghurt, to serve

1 Scrub the oranges and limes. Put the oranges in a large pot of boiling water and simmer for 1 hour. Add the limes and continue cooking for 1 hour more, or until all the fruit is very soft. Remove from the water and allow to cool. Cut the fruit in half, remove the seeds and discard. Put the remaining whole fruit, including the skins, into a blender or food processor and blend until smooth.

2 Preheat the oven to 190°C. Lightly spray a 22cm springform tin with canola spray and line it with paper.

3 Beat the eggs, egg whites, sugar and baking powder until thick and pale, then fold in the almond meal and citrus puree.

4 Spoon the mixture into the prepared tin and bake for 1 hour or until a skewer comes out clean when inserted in the centre.

5 Allow to cool in the tin. Serve with reduced fat ice-cream or yoghurt. Serves 8-10

NUTRIENTS per serve

Energy	752kJ
Energy	180cal
Total fat	14.0g
Saturated fat	1.3g
Monounsaturated fat	8.7g
Polyunsaturated fat	3.0g
Protein	8.3g
Carbohydrate	4.7g
Fibre	3.5g
Sodium	44mg
Cholesterol	54mg

Pear and Plum Crumble

PREP TIME **20 minutes** COOKING TIME **30 minutes**

4 firm beurre bosc pears
1 vanilla bean, cut in half lengthwise
2 tablespoons lemon juice
1/2 cup caster sugar
2 x 750g cans dark plums,
   drained and juice reserved

Crumble
1/3 cup rolled oats
1/2 cup plain flour
1/4 cup flaked almonds
1/3 cup brown sugar
50g polyunsaturated margarine

1 Preheat oven to 200°C. Peel and core the pears, then cut a thin slice off each of their bases so they sit flat.

2 Scrape the seeds out of the vanilla bean with a small knife. Put the seeds, scraped bean, lemon juice, sugar and 500ml water in a medium pot and stir over a low heat until the sugar dissolves. Bring to the boil, reduce the heat to barely a simmer and add the pears. Cook for 10 minutes or just until the pears are tender. Do not overcook or the pears will break up. Drain the pears, reserving 125ml of the liquid.

3 Stand each of the pears upright in a deep, 2 cup capacity ovenproof dish. Surround each pear with plums. Mix the reserved plum juice and pear cooking liquid and pour over the fruit in each dish.

4 To make the crumble   Put the oats, flour, almonds and sugar in a bowl and mix to combine. Rub the margarine gently into the dry ingredients, just until the texture becomes crumbly.

5 Sprinkle the crumble around each of the pears and over the plums. Put the dishes on a baking tray and cook for 20 minutes or until the crumble is crisp and golden.
Serves 4

NUTRIENTS per serve

Energy	2463kJ
Energy	597cal
Total fat	17.3g
Saturated fat	2.5g
Monounsaturated fat	7.2g
Polyunsaturated fat	6.3g
Protein	6.8g
Carbohydrate	102.8g
Fibre	11.0g
Sodium	112mg
Cholesterol	0mg

Steamed Banana and Maple Syrup Pudding

PREP TIME **30 minutes** COOKING TIME 1 hour 10 minutes

canola cooking spray
1/3 cup maple syrup
20g canola margarine
1 ripe banana, halved and quartered
250g pitted dates, chopped
1 whole star anise

1 teaspoon bicarbonate of soda
1 1/2 cups self-raising flour
1/2 cup dark brown sugar
2 eggs, lightly beaten
1 tablespoon safflower oil

NUTRIENTS per serve

Energy	1369kJ
Energy	327cal
Total fat	5.0g
Saturated fat	0.9g
Monounsaturated fat	2.4g
Polyunsaturated fat	1.2g
Protein	5.1g
Carbohydrate	67.0g
Fibre	4.4g
Sodium	232mg
Cholesterol	46mg

1 Put a trivet (small metal rack that protects the pudding basin from touching the hot base of the pot) in the bottom of a large pot. Put a 4 cup capacity pudding basin in the pot and pour enough cold water into the pot to come a third of the way up the side of the basin. Remove the basin and bring the measured water to the boil, reduce heat, cover and allow to simmer while preparing the pudding. Lightly spray the pudding basin with canola spray and line the base with a circle of non stick baking paper.
2 Heat the maple syrup and margarine in a small pot until the margarine melts then pour it into the basin. Arrange the banana, cut side down, in the bottom of the basin.
3 Put the dates and star anise in a small pot, add 250ml boiling water and boil until most of the liquid has been absorbed. Remove from the heat and stir in the bicarbonate of soda. Set aside and allow to cool slightly. Remove the star anise.
4 Sift the flour into a bowl and stir in the sugar. Make a well in the centre, stir in the cooled date mixture and the combined eggs and oil. Mix until smooth. Spoon the mixture into the prepared basin.
5 Cut a sheet each of baking paper and foil big enough to fit over the top and halfway down the side of the basin. Lay the paper on top of the foil and spray the paper with canola spray. Make a 1cm pleat down the centre of the foil and paper. Put the cover, paper side down and foil side up, on top of the basin and tie securely with string.
6 Carefully lower the pudding into the simmering water, put the lid on the pot and simmer for 1 hour or until a skewer comes out clean when inserted into the centre. Turn out onto a plate and serve warm with reduced fat custard. Serves 8

STAR INGREDIENT
BANANAS are a great healthy food choice when you need an energy boost. Nutritionally, they are high in carbohydrate, dietary fibre, vitamin C and potassium. Contrary to popular belief, they are not fattening.

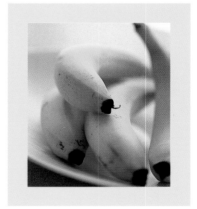

Ice-Cream Parfait

PREP TIME **15 minutes + chilling** COOKING TIME **5 minutes**

85g packet strawberry jelly crystals
500g strawberries
1 tablespoon icing sugar
500g reduced fat vanilla ice-cream or
  frozen vanilla yoghurt

100g amaretti (Italian bitter almond
  biscuits), crushed
2 tablespoons maple syrup
50g pistachio nuts, roughly chopped

1 Put the jelly crystals and 500ml boiling water in an ovenproof bowl and stir until the crystals dissolve. Refrigerate until set, then cut into small cubes.
2 Put 100g of the strawberries into a food processor or blender with the icing sugar and process until smooth.
3 Layer strawberries, strawberry puree, scoops of ice cream or frozen yoghurt, jelly and crushed amaretti into six tall parfait glasses. Finish with a drizzle of maple syrup and sprinkle with the chopped pistachio nuts. Serves 6

NUTRIENTS per serve

Energy	1141kJ
Energy	272cal
Total fat	4.5g
Saturated fat	0.6g
Monounsaturated fat	2.3g
Polyunsaturated fat	1.3g
Protein	9.0g
Carbohydrate	49.0g
Fibre	2.7g
Sodium	158mg
Cholesterol	5mg

TIP

Bread and butter pudding is usually high in fats - especially saturated fats - because it contains butter and full cream milk. This recipe is low in total and saturated fats, high in fibre and tastes just delicious!

Mango Bread and Butter Pudding

PREP TIME **20 minutes + standing** COOKING TIME **40 minutes**

canola cooking spray
1-2 large ripe mangoes, sliced or 400g can
  mangoes in natural juice, drained
1 loaf thick sliced, high-fibre white bread,
  (16 slices), toasted
2 eggs, lightly beaten

1/2 teaspoon ground cinnamon
1/2 cup caster sugar
250ml reduced fat milk or soy milk
1 tablespoon custard powder
reduced fat vanilla ice-cream or custard,
  to serve

1 Preheat oven to 180°C. Lightly spray four 1 cup capacity ramekins with canola spray and line the bases with a circle of non stick baking paper. Decoratively arrange some of the mango slices in the base of each ramekin.
2 Trim the crusts from the toast. Using a ramekin as a guide, cut bread rounds to fit into the dishes. Layer two slices of bread, then a layer of mango in each of the ramekins, then another two layers of bread, pressing down firmly between each layer.
3 Put the eggs, cinnamon, sugar, milk and custard powder in a jug and whisk to combine. Gradually pour the custard mixture into each ramekin and allow to stand for 10 minutes or until the bread has absorbed the custard.
4 Bake for 30-40 minutes or until the custard has set. Remove and allow to stand for 10 minutes before turning out onto serving plates. Serve with reduced fat vanilla ice-cream or reduced fat custard. Serves 4

NUTRIENTS per serve

Energy	1541kJ
Energy	368cal
Total fat	6.1g
Saturated fat	2.6g
Monounsaturated fat	1.9g
Polyunsaturated fat	0.7g
Protein	9.7g
Carbohydrate	70.0g
Fibre	3.2g
Sodium	248mg
Cholesterol	98mg

Rhubarb and Apple Pie with Vanilla Custard

PREP TIME **20 minutes** COOKING TIME **45 minutes**

TIP
A sweet treat is a perfect way to end a meal but it does not necessarily have to be high in fat. Fruit-based desserts are ideal as they tend to be lower in saturated fat and higher in fibre. So let your imagination run wild with fresh, dried or canned fruit-based desserts.

1kg Granny Smith apples, peeled, cored and cut into thick slices
1 cinnamon stick
1 cup caster sugar
1kg rhubarb, cut into 5cm lengths
1 sheet canola puff pastry, defrosted
3 tablespoons granulated sugar

Vanilla bean custard
1 tablespoon custard powder
500ml low or reduced fat milk
1/4 cup caster sugar
1 vanilla bean, cut in half lengthwise

1 Preheat oven to 200°C.
2 Put the apples, cinnamon stick and half the caster sugar in a pot. Add 60ml water, cover and cook over a medium heat for 10 minutes or until the apples are soft. Remove the cinnamon stick.
3 Put the rhubarb in a clean pot, add the remaining sugar and 60ml water and cook over a medium heat for 5-10 minutes or until the rhubarb is soft. Do not overcook or it will lose its colour and collapse.
4 Combine the rhubarb and apple and pile into a 23cm pie dish. Brush the edges of the pie dish with a little water.
5 Cover the pie with the puff pastry, trim off any excess and press the edges to seal the pie. Cut a few steam holes in the top, brush the pastry with water and sprinkle with granulated sugar. Bake on a heated tray for 20 minutes or until the pastry is crisp and golden.
6 To make the custard Blend the custard powder with a little of the milk to form a smooth paste. Transfer to a pot, add the remaining milk, sugar and vanilla bean and cook, stirring constantly, over a medium heat until the custard boils and thickens. Remove the vanilla bean before serving. Serves 8

STAR INGREDIENT
VANILLA BEANS or pods are the fruit of a tropical orchid. To release their exquisite flavour simply cut a bean in half lengthwise, scrape out the black seeds and heat both the bean and seeds in milk to make custard. The bean should be removed before serving, but the tiny black seeds are eaten.

Dessert

Warm Spiced Fruit

PREP TIME 10 minutes + cooling COOKING TIME 10 minutes

200g fresh pineapple, chopped
250g strawberries, halved
1 mango, peeled and sliced
2 plums, cut into wedges
2 peaches, cut into wedges
200g green and black grapes, rinsed
560g can lychees, drained and syrup
    reserved

350ml sauternes or other dessert wine
1 cinnamon stick
1 vanilla bean, cut in half lengthwise
1 stalk lemon grass, halved
2 whole star anise
reduced fat ice-cream, to serve

1 Gently mix the prepared fruit together.
2 Put the fruit in a single glass serving dish or individual glasses. Cover with plastic wrap while preparing the syrup.
3 Put the reserved lychee juice, sauternes, cinnamon stick, vanilla bean, lemon grass and star anise in a pot and bring to the boil. Reduce the heat and simmer for 10 minutes. Remove from the heat and allow to cool.
4 Pour the cooled syrup over the fruit and allow to stand for 15 minutes. Remove the cinnamon stick, vanilla bean, lemon grass and star anise before serving. Serve with reduced fat ice-cream. Serves 4

Cherry Clafoutis

PREP TIME 20 minutes COOKING TIME 30 minutes

canola cooking spray
1/2 cup plain flour
1/3 cup caster sugar
2 eggs
1 egg white
250ml reduced fat milk

1 teaspoon vanilla extract
500g pitted cherries, drained
2 tablespoons icing sugar
reduced fat yoghurt or ice-cream to serve

1 Preheat oven to 170°C. Lightly spray 4 individual ceramic gratin dishes (17cm top x 3 cm deep) with canola spray.
2 Put flour, sugar, eggs, egg white, milk and vanilla into a food processor or blender and process for 1 minute. Divide the custard mixture among the 4 dishes.
3 Arrange cherries on top of the custard and bake the clafoutis for 25-30 minutes or until the tops are golden and the filling just set.
4 Dust with icing sugar and serve immediately. Serves 4

NUTRIENTS per serve

| --- | --- |
Energy	1370kJ
Energy	327cal
Total fat	0.5g
Saturated fat	0g
Monounsaturated fat	0g
Polyunsaturated fat	0g
Protein	4.2g
Carbohydrate	52.0g
Fibre	6.7g
Sodium	65mg
Cholesterol	0mg

TIP

If you're eating out and deciding on a dessert or cake choose a sponge, fruit cake, muffin, pancake or scone as they are generally cooked with less fat. Watch out for any fatty fillings and toppings though!

NUTRIENTS per serve

Energy	1393kJ
Energy	333cal
Total fat	6.2g
Saturated fat	1.5g
Monounsaturated fat	3.1g
Polyunsaturated fat	1.0g
Protein	8.6g
Carbohydrate	62.0g
Fibre	4.7g
Sodium	67mg
Cholesterol	94mg

Glossary

Angina is a temporary chest pain or discomfort resulting from a reduced blood supply to the heart muscle. Angina occurs because part of the heart is temporarily unable to get enough blood and oxygen to meet its needs, due to abnormally narrowed artery in the heart.

Antioxidants are substances that defuse or combat free radicals (see below). Several antioxidant examples include vitamin C, vitamin E, lycopene, carotenoids and selenium. Fruit and vegetables are particularly rich in antioxidants.

Blood pressure is the pressure of blood in the arteries as it is being pumped around the body by the heart. High blood pressure can lead to heart attack, stroke, heart failure or kidney disease.

Calcium is a mineral present in large amounts in dairy foods, such as milk, cheese and yoghurt. It is also found in calcium-fortified soy drinks, canned salmon with bones, oysters, almonds, sesame seeds and tahini.

Calorie (cal) is a term for the amount of energy released when a food is burned for fuel in the body. The metric term for calorie is kilojoule (kJ). One calorie equals 4.2 kilojoules.

Carbohydrates are found mainly in plant foods such as breads, cereals, vegetables, fruit and legumes. Carbohydrates are digested and absorbed at different rates. Food that is slowly digested is recommended.

Cardiovascular disease is the largest single cause of death in Australia. It comprises heart, stroke and blood vessel disease.

Carotene is a substance found in some food, which is converted to vitamin A in the body. There are three types: alpha, beta and gamma carotene. Beta carotene has the greatest level of vitamin A activity. The richest food sources of beta carotene include orange and yellow fruit and vegetables such as carrots, pumpkin, mangoes, oranges, mandarines, pawpaw, rockmelons, apricots and yellow peaches.

Cholesterol may be one of two different types:
a) Blood cholesterol is a fatty substance normally produced by the body and carried by the blood. There are two different types: LDL cholesterol (the bad cholesterol) and HDL cholesterol (the good cholesterol). High levels of LDL cholesterol and low levels of HDL cholesterol in the blood are risk factors for heart disease and atherosclerosis.
b) Dietary cholesterol is found only in animal food (offal, fatty meat and poultry, eggs, milk, cheese etc). A lot of dietary cholesterol may raise blood cholesterol, but it is the saturated fat in food (see below) that has the most powerful effect on raising blood cholesterol.

Dietary fibre is only found in plant food. It is the part of food not digested in the stomach and small intestine. A lot of the dietary fibre consumed is digested by bacteria in the large intestine. There are two different types of fibre:
a) Soluble fibre can help lower blood cholesterol levels by removing cholesterol from the intestinal tract. Major sources of soluble fibre include fresh and dried fruit, vegetables, oats, legumes and psyllium husks.
b) Insoluble fibre acts as a stool softener and helps prevent constipation. It is found in bread, cereals, fruit, vegetables, legumes, seeds and nuts.

Energy is the amount of kilojoules or calories eaten or used. A high energy food is a high kilojoule/calorie food.

Folic acid (folate) is a B vitamin found naturally in most plant food, especially green leafy and other vegetables (spinach, brussels sprouts, broccoli, asparagus, leek, cauliflower and cabbage); fruit (oranges, bananas and strawberries); wholegrain breads, cereals and legumes (peas, dried beans and lentils); nuts; and yeast extract. It can also be added to food products such as some breads and breakfast cereals.

Free radicals are unstable particles produced in body cells as a normal part of metabolism, and by exposure to sunlight, X-rays and pollutants such as tobacco smoke, car exhaust and ozone. Free radicals can cause damage to body cells in a number of ways so large amounts in the body are not desirable.

Heart attack is typically caused by a blood clot that suddenly blocks a coronary artery, cutting the blood supply to the heart muscle. This can result in heart muscle damage.

Hydrogenation is a chemical process which makes liquid oils more saturated and solid. This process not only increases the amount of saturated fat in the oil, but it also produces trans fats. Hydrogenated fats are commonly used by food manufacturers, such as in the production of biscuits, pastries, snack food and convenience food.

Hypertension is another word for high blood pressure. High blood pressure is a major risk factor for heart disease.

Iron is a mineral present in food in two main forms:

a) Haem iron is found in red meat, poultry and seafood. Haem iron is much better absorbed by the body than non-haem iron.
b) Non-haem iron is found in cereals, fruit, vegetables and legumes. Absorption of the iron found in these foods can be increased by adding a vitamin C-rich food to a meal, like fresh orange juice, or by adding a food rich in haem iron, such as lean beef or trim lamb.

Kilojoule (kJ) is a technical metric term for the amount of energy produced when a food is burned in the body (see calorie above).

Legume is the term that covers dried beans, peas and lentils. They are also known as pulses. Examples include kidney beans, chickpeas, split peas and baked beans.

Magnesium is a mineral found in wheat bran, oats, wholemeal bread, milk, chicken, meat, fish, shellfish, legumes, some fruit and vegetables, and nuts.

Monounsaturated fat is a type of fat that lowers total cholesterol and LDL (bad) cholesterol when eaten in place of saturated fat. Sources include monounsaturated margarines and spreads; olive, canola and peanut oils; avocado; nuts; and seeds.

Niacin is a B vitamin found in canned tuna, fish, chicken, rabbit, turkey, beef, pork, game meat, liver, kidney, peanuts, peanut butter, wholegrain food products and yeast extract.

Omega-3 fats (or omega-3 fatty acids) can be divided into two groups:
a) EPA (Eicosapentaenoic acid) and DHA (Docosahexaenoic acid) are types of omega-3 polyunsaturated fats found predominantly in fish, particularly oily fish such as salmon, sardines, mackerel, trevally and tuna.
b) ALA (Alpha Linolenic Acid) is a different type of omega-3 polyunsaturated fat. Canola and soybean oils, linseeds (flaxseeds) and walnuts are high in ALA.

Phosphorus is a mineral commonly found in pasta, rolled oats, milk, yoghurt, cheese, eggs, chicken, beef, fish, shellfish, lamb, pork, dried beans, lentils, nuts and some vegetables.

Phytoestrogens are plant chemicals that have a similar structure to that of the human hormone oestrogen. Phytoestrogens behave like weak oestrogens. They are found in a variety of food including soy drinks, soy yoghurt, soy flour, soybeans, roasted soy nuts, lentils, tofu, tempeh, miso, textured vegetable protein (TVP), chickpeas, broad beans and linseed meal.

Polyunsaturated fat is a type of fat that lowers total cholesterol, LDL (bad) cholesterol and triglycerides when eaten in place of saturated fat. Sources include polyunsaturated margarines and spreads, corn, safflower, soybean and sunflower oils, deep sea oily fish, shellfish, nuts and seeds.

Potassium is a mineral found in a lot of fresh and dried fruit and vegetables, chickpeas, baked beans, beef, fish, chicken, lamb, milk, cereals and grains.

Protein is a major component of food. Proteins are made up of smaller units called amino acids. There are 23 amino acids, eight of which are know as 'essential amino acids', meaning that they cannot be made in the body and must be derived from food.

Riboflavin is a B vitamin found in liver, kidney, dairy products, fish, meat, almonds, eggs, broccoli, peas, dried beans, yeast extract, fortified breakfast cereals and some other food.

Saturated fat is a type of fat that raises total cholesterol and LDL (bad) cholesterol levels. Sources include full-fat dairy products, cream, butter, copha, lard, ghee, pastries, cakes, biscuits, fatty meat, many takeaway food and convenience packet food.

Soy protein is the protein found in soybeans and soy products. Including soy protein in a diet low in saturated fat and cholesterol may reduce the risk of coronary heart disease.

Stroke occurs when an artery (blood vessel) supplying blood to a part of the brain becames blocked or bursts. As a result, that part of the brain is damaged because it is deprived of its vital blood supply.

Thiamin is a B vitamin found in wholegrain products (wholemeal pasta, brown rice, rolled oats, bulgar or cracked wheat, wholemeal bread), fortified breakfast cereals, pork, nuts, yeast extract and some other food.

Trans fats (or trans fatty acids) are a type of fat found in some food. They behave like saturated fat by increasing total cholesterol and LDL (bad) cholesterol. Trans fats have the added negative side effect of lowering HDL (good) cholesterol. Sources include meat fat, dairy food (including butter) and some hydrogenated margarines and oils.

Triglycerides are a type of fat carried in the blood. Too many triglycerides in the blood can increase the risk of heart disease.

Vitamin B6 is a B vitamin found in fish, lentils, beans, pork, poultry, beef, lamb, nuts, bananas, avocado and a variety of other fruit and vegetables.

Vitamin B12 is a B vitamin found mainly in animal food, particularly liver and kidney. It is also found in rabbit, duck, pork, beef, lamb, turkey, chicken, oysters and fish.

Vitamin C (ascorbic acid) is a water-soluble vitamin and antioxidant found in fresh fruit (especially citrus fruit, kiwifruit, guava, pawpaw and strawberries) and vegetables (especially capsicum, brussels sprouts, broccoli and cauliflower).

Vitamin E is a fat-soluble vitamin and antioxidant mainly found in oils like wheatgerm, sunflower, safflower, canola, corn, soybean and olive, as well as nuts and seeds. It is also found in some seafood.

Zinc is a mineral found in oysters, shellfish, dried beans, nuts, oats, bran, rice, wholemeal bread, beef, liver, pork and chicken.

About our recipes and 'nutrients per serve' tables

Each recipe has been carefully analysed by the Heart Foundation to ensure it complies with our healthy eating philosophy and meets our nutritional guidelines regarding fat (particularly the type of fat), sodium and fibre. We provide you with the nutritional details of each recipe in a 'nutrients per serve' table. The nutritional information provided is based on the recommended serving size per recipe, which is at the end of the cooking method for each recipe. Where a serving size refers to a range of serves (such as 4-6), the nutritional analysis details are based on the highest number of serves, in this case 6. Where a large number of serves or portions are mentioned (such as makes 12 muffins), the analysis is based on one serve or portion, in this case one muffin. Energy per serve is expressed in both kilojoules (kJ) and calories (cal). Other nutrients are in grams (g) or milligrams (mg). Accompaniments and garnishes, mentioned as a serving suggestion at the end of some recipes, are not included in the nutritional analysis. Preparation and cooking times are based on estimates of the time it would take a person who is familiar with cooking, but not an expert.
The times may vary according to your experience.

Imperial/metric Conversion Chart

Metric cup and spoon sizes

Measurements used in this book refer to the standard metric cup and spoon sets approved by the Standards Association of Australia. A basic metric cup set consists of: 1 cup, 1/2 cup, 1/3 cup and 1/4 cup sizes. The basic spoon set consists of: 1 tablespoon, 1 teaspoon, 1/2 teaspoon and 1/4 teaspoon sizes.
Note: Eggs are 48-50g each

Cup	Spoon
1/4 cup = 60ml	1/4 teaspoon = 1.25ml
1/3 cup = 80ml	1/2 teaspoon = 2.5ml
1/2 cup = 125ml	1 teaspoon = 5ml
1 cup = 250ml	1 tablespoon = 20ml

Liquids

Imperial	Metric	Metric
1 fl oz	-	30ml
2 fl oz	1/4 cup	60ml
3 fl oz	-	100ml
4 fl oz	1/2 cup	125ml
5 fl oz	-	150ml
6 fl oz	3/4 cup	200ml
8 fl oz	1 cup	250ml
10 fl oz	1 1/4 cups	300ml
12 fl oz	1 1/2 cups	375ml
14 fl oz	1 3/4 cups	425ml
15 fl oz	-	475ml
16 fl oz	2 cups	500ml
20 fl oz (1 pint)	2 1/2 cups	600ml

Mass (weight)

Approximate conversion for cookery purposes

Imperial	Metric	Imperial	Metric
1/2oz	15g	10oz	300g
1oz	30g	11oz	345g
2oz	60g	12oz (3/4lb)	375g
3oz	90g	13oz	410g
4oz (1/4lb)	125g	14oz	440g
5oz	155g	15oz	470g
6oz	185g	16oz (1lb)	500g (0.5kg)
7oz	220g	24oz (1 1/2lb)	750g
8oz (1/2lb)	250g	32oz (2lb)	1000g (1kg)
9oz	280g	3lb	1500g (1.5kg)

Oven temperatures

Oven	Celsius	Fahrenheit
Very slow	120	250
Slow	140-150	275-300
Moderately slow	160	325
Moderate	180	350
Moderately hot	190	375
Hot	200-230	400-450
Very hot	250-260	475-500

Note: Set fan ovens at about 20° Celsius below the stated temperature.

Index

Heart Foundation

About the Heart Foundation

Every year thousands of Australian families are devastated by the traumatic loss of a loved one to heart attack or stroke.

The Heart Foundation is committed to improving the heart health of all Australians and to reducing disability and premature death from heart attack, stroke and related diseases.

The Heart Foundation is one of Australia's leading independent non-profit organisations and is funded almost entirely by donations from the public and gifts in wills. Since we began our work over 40 years ago, the risk of dying from heart attack, stroke or related diseases has more than halved.

The Heart Foundation funds individual researchers, many amongst the best young scientists in Australia. Thanks to the incredible generosity of the Australian public, we have been able to invest more than $140 million into life-saving heart research. Demand for quality research, however, exceeds our funding resources and we can currently only fund one in five research projects.

The Heart Foundation is also working across a large number of areas to improve heart health, including programs in nutrition, physical activity, support of cardiac rehabilitation, tobacco control and in rural and remote health.

The Challenge Ahead

Despite our success, cardiovascular disease is still this country's biggest killer, causing more than one in three Australian deaths each year.

Over 80 percent of the adult population have at least one of the following cardiovascular risk factors: tobacco smoking, poor nutrition, physical inactivity, high blood pressure or overweight.

Thanks to the Heart Foundation much has been learnt about heart disease, but there is so much more to discover. We still don't fully understand, for example, what makes certain people more prone to heart attacks than others.

Help us...

By purchasing this cookbook, you are already directly helping our fight against heart disease. As a non-profit organisation, with almost no government funding, we need your help in many simple ways. These include recommending this cookbook to your friends; participating in Heart Foundation community events; and making a donation or leaving a gift to the Heart Foundation in your will.

...to help you

The Heart Foundation is committed to providing the most accurate, up-to-date information for everyone concerned about their heart health. For the cost of a local call you can ring HEARTLINE and talk to our health professionals about any heart health issue including cholesterol, healthy eating, physical activity, heart surgery procedures and more.

Call 1300 36 27 87 today.

Heart Foundation contact details

New South Wales

Sydney
407 Elizabeth Street
Surry Hills NSW 2010
Phone (02) 9219 2444

Newcastle
Suite 5, OTP House
Bradford Close
Kotara NSW 2289
Phone (02) 4952 4699

Queensland

Brisbane
557 Gregory Terrace
Fortitude Valley QLD 4006
Phone (07) 3854 1696

Rockhampton
Unit 6, 160 Bolsover Street
Rockhampton QLD 4700
Phone (07) 4922 2195

Toowoomba
417 Ruthven Street
Toowoomba QLD 4350
Phone (07) 4632 3673

Townsville
36 Gregory Street
Townsville QLD 4810
Phone (07) 4721 4686

South Australia

155-159 Hutt Street
Adelaide SA 5000
Phone (08) 8224 2888

ACT

Cnr Denison Street & Geils Court
Deakin ACT 2600
Phone (02) 6282 5744

Tasmania

86 Hampden Road
Battery Point TAS 7000
Phone (02) 6224 2722

Victoria

411 King Street
West Melbourne VIC 3003
Phone (03) 9329 8511

Western Australia

334 Rokeby Road
Subiaco WA 6008
Phone (08) 9388 3343

Northern Territory

Third Floor
Darwin Central Building
21 Knuckey Street
Darwin NT 0800
Phone (08) 8981 1966

Heart Foundation website
www.heartfoundation.com.au
Heartline 1300 36 27 87
Donation line 1300 55 02 82